Student-Generated RUBRICS

An Assessment Model to Help All Students Succeed

Larry Ainsworth and Jan Christinson

from the Assessment Bookshelf series
Dale Seymour Publications®
Orangeburg, New York

We respectfully and gratefully dedicate this book to Jane Cimolino, our mentor, and Carol Herrera, our principal. Special thanks to the original fifth-grade team members: Jane Cimolino, Shane Little, Kimberly Baker, and Scott Koopsen. Thanks also to teacher Sherry Lawson in Coronado, California, for sharing her Problem of the Week Guide; to Julie Salley for her contributions to the project; and to Leigh Childs for her guidance and inspiration.

Managing Editor: Catherine Anderson
Production/Manufacturing Director: Janet Yearian
Project Editor: Joan Gideon
Production Coordinator: Joe Conte
Text Design: Polly Christensen
Cover Design: Don Taka
Cover Photos: Comstock, Inc.

Published by Dale Seymour Publications®, an imprint of Addison Wesley Longman, Inc.

Dale Seymour Publications
125 Greenbush Road South
Orangeburg, New York 10962
Customer Service: 800-872-1100

Order Number DS21855

ISBN 1-57232-921-1

1 2 3 4 5 6 7 8 9 10-VG-01 00 99 98 97

Contents

Introduction:
Sharing the Experience

In January 1995, we were invited by the San Diego County Office of Education coordinators for the California Assessment Collaborative to present a workshop to their Assessment Leadership Academy. In this workshop, titled "Setting Standards Together," we shared practical, effective strategies for implementing an assessment process that involved students as well as teachers. We also displayed examples of task-specific performance standards on which students and teachers collaborated. Workshop participants embraced this assessment format, and since then we have shared this model in school districts throughout California and Arizona.

Teachers invariably recognize the validity of an assessment method that has been used effectively by teachers in the classroom. As we have continued to present our model to groups of teachers, we have come to realize the applicability of this method of assessment across all grades and subject areas. *Student-Generated Rubrics: An Assessment Model to Help All Students Succeed* will give you an alternative assessment program that is presented clearly enough to implement immediately in your own classroom.

Though some chapters give examples from primary classrooms and others refer to intermediate classrooms, all teachers should read all chapters. By understanding the important role primary teachers play in introducing their students to writing rubrics and to self-assessing, intermediate teachers can build upon that foundation. Likewise, primary teachers can better prepare their students by becoming familiar with the more sophisticated rubrics developed in upper grades, which measure quality as well as content and require both peer assessment and self-assessment. The power of this model increases when primary and intermediate teachers fit all the individual parts together to create an exciting, schoolwide instruction and assessment program. Sample focus questions, performance tasks, and student-generated performance standards as well as actual work completed by students can be found in chapter 15 and throughout the book.

We hope that you will complete the Reader's Assignments at the end of each chapter; they will help you implement this program in your own classroom. As you use this assessment model, your students will become increasingly involved in evaluating the quality and content of their own and others' work, and they will be motivated to do well.

Assessment of Performance Tasks

Part of the educational-reform movement sweeping the nation is the call to redesign the evaluation of student performance. Most teachers, parents, and administrators are not content to measure student learning using only standardized, norm-referenced tests. Even though standardized tests provide objective data that can be quantified and compared, they do not require students to apply what they have learned.

Alternative Assessment and Authentic Assessment

Assessment is *authentic* when it closely matches instruction and involves students in the kinds of projects they will find in real life. Educators today realize that authentic assessment must be part of the overall evaluation of student progress. Traditional assessment tests, which can be scored on a percentage basis and are easy to administer and grade, are a legitimate part of student evaluation. But it is also important to assess projects to which students apply what they have learned.

Unlike traditional assessment (i.e. tests), *alternative* assessment encompasses a broad range of activities that provide in-depth information about students' progress. It evaluates many student outputs, such as posters, journals, student-made videos, and group projects. Student processes—including how students work in groups and how they solve problems—are also assessed.

Performance Tasks

Projects assigned for the purpose of assessing student understanding are known as *performance tasks.* A performance task does not resemble a traditional test in any way, yet its purpose is the same: to find out what students comprehend about what has been taught. Performance tasks challenge the teacher to creatively design a different format for evaluating student understanding.

Teachers who use performance tasks often prefer them to tests because these tasks allow students to demonstrate a much wider and richer level of understanding. For example, fourth-grade students making a salt-and-flour relief map of their state would demonstrate knowledge of the geographical regions by shaping each region with dough and then painting those regions different colors. Fifth-grade students studying the Plains Indians of North America might stage a videotaped newscast in which they show they have met the unit's learning objectives. The relief map and the video newscast are performance tasks, and in each example, students show their level of understanding through what they create.

Grading Performance Tasks

Grading performance tasks requires a clear set of criteria. *Rubrics,* brief outlines that describe the content and quality needed to achieve a specific grade, help the grader determine the evidence of students' understanding and communication of that understanding. Often the rubric is divided into numerical levels of achievement—three levels for primary grades and four or six levels for intermediate and secondary grades.

Many *general scoring rubrics* provide teachers with a generic standard for evaluating performance tasks. General rubrics often use ambiguous phrases such as *completely fulfills* and *adequately describes* to define each score point. These terms or labels may be interpreted differently by different people. If assessment is to be valid and reliable, it must be objective. Teachers, students, and parents must be able to determine precisely which criteria are required for each performance level.

Task-specific rubrics list the precise criteria for a specific performance task. Such rubrics take the mystery out of grading for teachers and students alike. By using task-specific rubrics,

- ambiguity of grading is eliminated
- reliability and validity of scoring are significantly increased
- objectivity in assessing subjective student work is achieved

When students are actively involved in establishing grading criteria, task-specific rubrics become even more effective. Under the direction of the teacher, students determine the specific language and evaluation descriptors for each score *before* they begin the performance task. Thus students agree that the task-specific rubric generated is clear and fair, and they follow its guidelines as they complete the project. Because they set the standards, students take pride in their work, are motivated to do well, and experience ownership of the entire learning and assessment process.

Background of This Assessment Model

This model of assessment was initially developed by a team of fifth-grade teachers from three elementary schools in the Carlsbad Unified School District (California). Working with Principal Carol Herrera (Kelly School, Carlsbad), the team wrote learning objectives for integrating social studies and language arts and then planned units of study to match the objectives.

During the first year, the team met weekly to share their own successes, frustrations, and discoveries, and any modifications they had made in implementing the model within their own classroom. The teachers' primary function was to guide students through this assessment process by modeling and giving clarification as needed. This was often challenging, as teachers encountered their own individual learning curves while working with students. Teachers found that their weekly meetings were a valuable forum where exchanging ideas led to their own professional growth.

The team listed the following sequence of steps to guide them in instruction and assessment.

1. *The teacher establishes the focus questions.* The teacher first identifies focus questions for the unit—the three or four major learning objectives students are to meet. These can be thought of as the "big ideas" students should walk away with when the unit is completed. Focus questions guide both instruction and assessment. Thus the assessment will be

deliberately aligned with the instructional objectives of the unit. Once these focus questions are identified, the teacher shares them with her students. The teacher and her students then know where they are headed as they study the unit.

2. *The teacher selects a performance task.* The teacher selects a unit project that will give students the opportunity to demonstrate their understanding of the focus questions.
3. *The teacher chooses learning activities to match the focus questions.* Once the instructional focus of the unit is decided, the team of teachers selects activities and lessons for the unit. Referring to the focus questions helps the teacher determine which activities will advance student understanding of the unit themes.
4. *Students and their teacher create a task-specific rubric.* Prior to beginning their work on the unit project, students help create a task-specific scoring rubric to evaluate this unit performance task. As students create their projects, there is no mystery about what is required or how their work will be graded. Nor is there any question about the meaning or validity of the grading rubric.
5. *Students conduct self-assessment and peer assessment.* When the performance task is complete, students evaluate their own work and the work of their peers using the published classroom rubric. Any student who does not agree with the peer-assessment grade can appeal the grade to the teacher. Any appeal has to be based upon the rubric's criteria.
6. *The teacher determines the final grade.* Once all student assessments are complete, the teacher reviews them and determines the final grade for each project.
7. *Students reflect on their performance.* As the final step, students reflect on their progress. They compile unit folders, share these unit folders with their parents (who may choose to add comments), and return them to the teacher, who places them in their learning portfolios.

2

Rubrics: General and Task-Specific

Many general rubrics have been published, and we've provided a sample of one below. Even though some educators, students, and parents could pick up a student's writing project and categorize it as *Wow, Pretty Good,* or *Needs Work* according to the descriptors below, there is a problem. Look again at the subjective language: *Showing* means using descriptive writing to paint a picture in the reader's mind rather than just stating something. (This tells: "It was a hot day." This shows: "Perspiration dripped down his neck. Everywhere people were sitting listlessly fanning themselves.") What is *lots* of showing? Must the writing be interesting to *everyone*? How much is *most*?

Wow	Pretty Good	Needs Work
• Lots of showing • Interesting to read • Clear story	• A little showing • Most parts are interesting • Most of it is clear • Handwriting is easy to read • A few spelling errors	• No showing • Not very interesting • Many confusing parts

This rubric is ambiguous. One person's interpretation of almost any of the descriptors may differ greatly from another's. Professional educators might be able to reach a consensus for most papers, but there would certainly be those fence-sitter papers that some teachers would classify as *Wow* and others would see as only *Pretty Good.* And if trained teachers can't always agree, how much harder would it be for students to use these general descriptions to evaluate their own work and their peers' work?

A Personal Experience with General Rubrics

In the summer of 1994, we were both selected—along with nearly a hundred other educators—to score the math portion of the fourth-grade California Learning Assessment Program (CLAS) test in San Diego, California. Each of us sat with five other teacher-readers and a trained table leader. Before ever being allowed to score actual student papers, we were intensively trained to calibrate. *Calibrate,* in this sense, means that any teacher-reader's score of a particular student paper would match that of any other teacher-reader's score of the same paper.

We were provided with *anchor papers,* or benchmarks, for each numerical score point, against which we were to measure student papers to determine a calibrated score. The rubric we used, which was developed by the California Department of Education, is shown here.

CLAS Mathematics Open-Ended Scoring Guide

4 Fully Accomplishes Purpose of Task	3 Substantially Accomplishes Purpose of Task	2 Partially Accomplishes Purpose of Task	1 Makes Little or No Progress Toward Accomplishing Purpose of Task
• Student work shows full grasp of the central math ideas. • Recorded work communicates clear thinking, using some combination of written, symbolic, or visual means.	• Student work shows essential grasp of the central math ideas. • Recorded work in large part communicates the thinking.	• Student work shows partial but limited grasp of the central math ideas. • Recorded work is incomplete, misdirected, or not clearly presented.	• Student work shows little or no grasp of the central math ideas. • Recorded work is barely (if at all) comprehensible.

Our first practice round of scoring went fairly well. We had before us anchor papers for each score point and an *essence statement* that contained the essential mathematics of the problem students had solved. We continually reviewed these documents as we assigned scores to the practice papers we had been given. Our table leader would then conduct her own *read-behind assessment,* or double-checking of the scores we had posted, to determine whether or not we had calibrated successfully. Those of us who were successful moved into the next training phase. Those who were not were accompanied to another room for further training. We jokingly referred to this as "being sent to the office."

We were then introduced to *range-finders.* These were sample student papers that seemed difficult to classify. At first glance, a paper might appear to be a 3 but after a second reading become a 4, or vice versa. Sometimes we could not decide whether a paper merited a 2 or a 3. Again and again, we were directed to study the rubric and the essence statement to assist us in making a decision.

Our table leaders were busy conducting read-behinds, alerting us to how many papers we had calibrated successfully and how many we had assigned an adjacent score (one score point off) or worse, a discrepant score (two points off the mark). If you accumulated too many discrepant scores, you were tapped on the shoulder and sent to the office!

Finding Ambiguity in the Rubric

Look closely at each of the CLAS rubric classifications and their descriptors. Do you notice any ambiguity? Can you distinguish between *fully accomplishes* and *substantially accomplishes*? Where is the distinction between *full grasp of central math ideas* to earn a 4 versus *essential grasp of central math ideas* to score a 3?

Although we found the CLAS scoring process ambiguous at times, we both look back on that experience as one of the most beneficial in our professional lives because it challenged us to develop a workable method of evaluating performance tasks. For the first time, we realized that evaluation of performance tasks should be organized, valid, and reliable—and that it should make sense to all who looked at the task.

The training and grading of CLAS tests challenged us to find a way to make rubrics specific enough that teachers, students, and parents would know precisely the required criteria for each performance level.

In our workshops with teachers, we usually end our discussion of general rubrics with this scenario:

Your children ask to go out on a Saturday night. You tell them they must clean their rooms to determine their own curfew times as follows:

Fully Accomplished: You may stay out until 2 A.M.

Substantially Accomplished: You may stay out until midnight.

Partially Accomplished: You must clean your room better before you go out.

No Progress: You will stay home with Mom and Dad on Saturday night.

There is always laughter, especially from those workshop participants with teenagers. We then ask, "What problems might occur in using this rubric with your own children?" Invariably we hear, "What *fully* means to my kid is not what it means to me!" The subsequent discussion always points out the need to show the child exactly what the parent's definition of a clean room is.

Writing a Task-Specific Rubric

The teachers are then given their first task-specific rubric writing assignment: "Working with those at your table, please come up with specific descriptors for each of the above four clean-room categories, and be prepared to share the rubric you create with the whole group." Here is how far one group went in order to guarantee a room that met their standards of cleanliness.

Rubric for Cleaning Your Room			
Fully Accomplished	**Substantially Accomplished**	**Partially Accomplished**	**No Progress**
• Bed perfectly made (linens tucked in; bedspread smooth with pillow in correct position under bedspread) • Closet clean and organized (all clothing on hangers; no junk on closet floor) • Bookshelves and countertops dusted and free of clutter • Dresser drawers neatly organized and closed • Walls free of dirt • Floor free of clutter and vacuumed • Trash can emptied and all messes removed • Shoes lined up in matched pairs	• Bed made (linens under bedspread and not visible) • Closet generally clean and organized (most clothing on hangers; little or no clutter on closet floor) • Bookshelves and countertops not dusted, but items on them look tidy • Dresser drawers organized and closed • Walls free of fingerprints and most smudges • Floor free of most clutter and ready to be vacuumed • Trash can emptied and most messes removed	• Bedspread pulled up over lumpy and visible sheets, blanket, and pillow • Closet neither clean nor organized • Bookshelves and countertops piled with stuff • Dresser drawers closed but bursting with unfolded, unmatched clothing • Floor covered with clutter, except for narrow walking path to bed • Trash can not emptied and some messes remain	• "Is there a bed under this?" • "I can't even see the floor!"

Is the expected performance clear to you after reading this rubric? Our guess is that almost anyone could recognize a clean room with this degree of specificity. Simply stated, the point is this: Task-specific rubrics demystify the grading process when students are involved in the evaluation of performance tasks.

3 Focus Questions to Guide Instruction and Assessment

Good instruction should begin with the end goals clearly in mind. When planning a unit of study, teachers striving for curriculum alignment—the matching of the curriculum to the material on which students will be tested—should do the following:

- Identify the learning objectives—the essential knowledge and understanding students need to acquire based on district guidelines and state frameworks.
- Design lessons around those learning objectives.
- Select a performance task that accurately measures student performance in relation to the objectives.

The learning objectives are summarized in the *focus questions*—the three or four major ideas that guide instruction toward assessment.

Developing Focus Questions

When planning a unit, teachers in grade-level teams typically discuss and agree upon the unit's big ideas. We often think of the big ideas as learning objectives written simply enough for students to immediately understand what is required. Clearly stating focus questions is critical to any method of student-generated evaluation. Students should see the big ideas, or *focus questions,* as the main things they will learn, remember, and do at the conclusion of the unit. Before students can understand a unit's big ideas, teachers need to personally identify them, either individually, with another teacher, or with a grade-level team.

Intermediate teacher Jane Cimolino, our mentor throughout the process of learning to use student-generated rubrics, taught us to clarify a unit's objectives and put them in the language a student can easily understand. We found that to start by identifying big ideas led naturally to selecting a performance task and lessons and activities that accomplished the identified learning outcomes.

It is often true that teachers find it is easier to identify focus questions when they work with a colleague or grade-level team. The collaborative process is helpful because it clarifies the unit goals and keeps them clear to the teacher. These goals are stated and explained to students at the beginning of the unit, so everyone knows exactly what learning is to take place.

Here are three focus questions developed for a fifth-grade social studies unit on the land bridge across the Bering Strait:

1. How and why did people come to North America?
2. What evidence do we have for our theories?
3. How and where did the land bridge form?

Matching Performance Tasks to Focus Questions

Once teachers determine the focus questions and the performance task, they share them with students and post them in the classroom for the duration of the unit. This ensures that all participants understand the goals of the unit and how work will be assessed.

As instruction progresses, teachers use the focus questions to periodically review content and check student understanding. For example, after the first two weeks of a new unit, students might take a quiz, engage in a discussion, or complete a writing activity that addresses one or more of the focus questions. The performance task for the above unit on the land bridge across the Bering Strait might require students to write a five-paragraph essay in which each of the three body paragraphs answers one of the three focus questions.

Although it can be challenging to write focus questions for an integrated unit with extensive content, you'll find that focus questions make planning easier, help you sift through the many activities from the various content areas, and simplify the selection of a performance task that spans the breadth of content.

Identifying unit focus questions is an essential step in our model of assessment. Focus questions

- streamline the entire instructional process
- match the performance task to the unit objectives
- keep students focused on the stated goals of the unit
- give teachers a handle on the amount of curriculum there is to cover

The more we use this instruction and assessment model in our own classroom programs, the more we see the value of focus questions. The concept may seem simple, even obvious, but the result is amazing. It is much more than curricular alignment; it takes learning to the next level.

By identifying the essential learning you want to take place, you lead students to a deeper level of understanding through instruction and activities. With a clear focus for each unit, you spend less time trying to do *everything* in that unit and can move on to the essential ideas in other units.

Identify the big ideas you want students to retain. If you do this for each unit you plan, you will soon see how this process increases student learning and decreases teacher burnout!

Reader's Assignment: Write four focus questions for your favorite unit.

4

Choosing the Performance Task

What is performance? According to Grant Wiggins, executive director of Consultants on Learning Assessment and School Structure and a leading authority on assessment,

> The word *perform* in common parlance means to execute a task or process and to bring it to completion. Our ability to perform with knowledge can therefore be assessed only as we produce some work of our own, using a repertoire of knowledge and skills and being responsive to the particular tasks and contexts at hand ("Assessment: Authenticity, Context, and Validity," *Phi Delta Kappan* [November 1993]: 202).

Performance-based assessment tasks differ from traditional tests in that the focus is on full demonstration of student learning acquired from all unit activities and instruction. They offer students the opportunity to display both breadth and depth of the content that they've learned and that is relevant to the instructional goals of the unit. Performance tasks are designed to allow student work to be evaluated for both content and quality of presentation.

Designing Performance Tasks

In *Authentic Assessment* (Menlo Park, Calif.: Addison-Wesley, 1994), author Diane Hart writes

> Designing performance tasks is a challenge. Good tasks grow out of the curriculum. They are feasible in terms of available time and resources. They are inviting to both teachers and students. And the results can be scored and reported in ways that satisfy students, teachers, parents, administrators, as well as district or state testing directors.

What should a performance task look like?

- The task should do what its name implies—measure performance related to the stated unit goals.
- It should be in a student-friendly format similar to the learning activities students encountered during the unit.
- The task should afford all students the opportunity to show their learning relative to the focus questions.

We have found this third point to be very important. In any classroom, there is a wide spectrum of ability levels among students. Well-designed performance tasks afford the opportunity for all students to be successful relative to their current performance levels. Students identified as gifted can demonstrate the full range of their understanding as they complete the task requirements. Special-needs students can experience success by demonstrating understanding that appears more basic but nonetheless fulfills the task requirements. Second-language learners, when they understand the task and receive clear language and writing assistance, will also be able to represent their grasp of the content.

Helpful Guidelines and Other Considerations

Here are three simple but helpful guidelines offered by Michael Hibbard in his article "On the Cutting Edge of Assessment" (*ASCD Education Update* 38 [June 1996]: 4) to assist all classroom teachers in the design of performance tasks.

- What do we want kids to know and be able to do?
- How well do we want them to be able to do it?
- What does quality look like?

For a unit that integrates several subject areas, the performance task should encompass the subject-specific goals (focus questions) of each content area. For example, an integrated performance task such as the video newscast mentioned in chapter 3 would include oral language, written language, and social studies content in a group-presentation format.

The format of the performance tasks can and should be varied throughout the year to keep students (and teachers) motivated. For example, assign book reports in different formats for each genre of literature: a hanging mobile for science fiction, a bio-poem for biographies, a haunted-house poster with clues in the windows for mysteries, and so on. Varying the performance tasks throughout the year accommodates differing learning styles and enables all students to succeed.

The Power of Collaboration

The team of fifth-grade teachers that launched this model of assessment discovered the tremendous benefit of collaborating—especially when designing performance tasks. These are the steps they followed in that collaboration process.

1. Individual teachers shared favorite unit activities from prior years.
2. The team analyzed activities to determine whether student understanding could be shown in various ways.
3. The team selected the activity that was best suited to become a performance task.
4. The team modified the performance task to fit the focus questions.

Assessment Comes in Many Forms

Teachers in our workshop presentations often ask us whether we use performance tasks as our only means of assessment. We explain that we use performance tasks only with big projects or as culminating activities for units. We recognize the value of using a wide variety of assessment measures, including more traditional tests, to showcase student understanding in as many ways as possible.

Reader's Assignment: Develop a performance task for your favorite unit.

5 Teaching Students to Write Rubrics

You've identified your focus questions for the unit, you've carefully selected a performance task that will allow students to demonstrate the full range of their understanding, and you've presented these to your students. Now what?

It's time to determine how student work will be assessed and to share that information with students *before* they begin working. The best way to do this is to have students create the grading standards with you.

A set of grading criteria is now commonly referred to as a *rubric.* The key distinction in our definition of a rubric is that it is task-specific and that students are involved in determining the language descriptors for content and quality. We strongly believe that using commercially produced or general rubrics that contain subjective terms makes it difficult for students to assess their own work and the work of others. Task-specific rubrics, authored collaboratively by students and their teacher, clarify the criteria used to evaluate the project. Because students are directly involved in establishing these criteria, they understand them thoroughly and can apply them.

Steps in Building the Rubric with Students

When generating rubrics with students, we typically follow these steps to create a class-authored rubric. (Each of these steps will be explained more fully in the next two chapters.)

1. Explain and clarify the performance task and how it matches the focus questions.
2. Show sample student projects from prior years (if available).
3. Explain the benefits of a task-specific rubric.
4. Show a prior year's rubric (if available).

5. Begin writing the rubric. Use task requirements as baseline criteria.
6. Elicit student suggestions for quality and content descriptors.
7. Ensure, through teacher-student discussion, that students understand the rubric language.
8. Record student responses, and facilitate classroom consensus of rubric terms. Clarify any terms that seem subjective or ambiguous.
9. Follow the process for each score point.
10. Review, revise, and edit the final rubric.
11. Publish the rubric.
12. Send the rubric home to parents.

Thoughts to Consider

We have listed here a few important suggestions to help you as you begin to use this model of assessment in your own classroom.

- *Value the discussion.* The discussion generated when you're setting grading criteria is invaluable because subjective terms or descriptors are objectified and made clear to everyone involved.
- *Start with simple rubrics: 1, 2, 3 or A, B, C.* Five- or six-point rubrics are difficult to design and use effectively. The more grade points a rubric has, the more difficult the grading process becomes.
- *Only use rubrics with major projects or activities.* The rubric process should be only one part of a comprehensive assessment program.
- *Start with the curricular area you feel is your strongest subject.* It is much easier to design your first rubric for a content area you feel confident teaching.
- *Work with another teacher.* Like most new ventures, the rubric-writing process can be frustrating initially. Implementing student-generated rubrics for the first time may be easier if you collaborate with another teacher.

- *Be patient. Rubrics don't have to be perfect!* Give yourself and your students permission to experiment with this process.
- *This process works in both graded and developmental classroom settings.* We have seen this model used effectively in secondary-level, single-subject classrooms, in special-education programs, and at the kindergarten–lower-primary level, where the assessment emphasis is developmental in nature.
- *It is easier the next time around.* Students get better at writing rubrics over time. Students experienced at writing rubrics can model the process for other students, which will increase student participation and produce better rubrics.

In the forthcoming chapters, we will show how rubrics were generated by students under the direction of their teachers in an intermediate and a primary classroom. We re-create discussions teachers had with their students. In some instances, we have included some of the insights we've gained.

Reader's Assignment: Write a simple rubric by yourself or with your team members for the performance task you developed in chapter 4.

Writing a Rubric in the Intermediate Classroom

When we share this assessment model in professional development workshops, the participating teachers show heightened interest when we begin showing the work our own students have produced. Our focus shifts from describing the model to our own actual experience with it. It is this sharing—teacher to teacher—that convinces them the model is more than an interesting concept.

In this chapter, Larry Ainsworth relates his experience implementing this method of student-generated assessment in his own classroom.

Our First Rubric Matched to Focus Questions

Jane Cimolino and I had begun the planning discussion for the science component of our prehistoric unit with this question: "What do we want students to know about prehistoric animals?" These are the focus questions we generated.

1. What did prehistoric animals look like?
2. Where and when did they live?
3. What was their diet and their habitat?
4. What interesting facts can we find about their enemies, life span, height, and so on?

Start with a C

Jane had told me to start with the C category first, to establish a baseline criteria of requirements for the performance-task assignment. We were beginning the science component of our prehistoric unit. In this unit, students in cooperative groups had to research information on a prehistoric animal, create a poster about that animal, and present the poster to the class.

There I stood in front of my sixth-grade class, ready to lead my new students through our first rubric-writing process. With marker in hand and a clean sheet of paper on the easel, I was entering brand-new territory. My colleagues Jan Christinson and Jane Cimolino had outlined for me all the basics, but I had never written a rubric either on my own or with other teachers. I was eager to try it!

So I asked the kids, "What would a C poster look like? What words or phrases should we include? Let's look at our focus questions to help us get started."

Evan's hand shot up. "There should be a large title of the animal," he said, "and the names of the students in the group." Mai volunteered to be our recorder so I could concentrate on leading the classroom discussion. I asked her to write down Evan's suggestion.

Michelle raised her hand. "They should tell about the animal's habitat and diet," she said. Mai added that to the list. Darnell said, "There should be two interesting facts and some kind of picture." Mai looked at me, I nodded, and she recorded it.

I kept looking at the focus questions and the kids caught on to my intent. Soon the C criteria directly matched the focus questions. I asked the class the obvious question, "Do you see the relationship between the focus questions and our C criteria?" Well, of course they did, but it still seemed pretty impressive to them. "Should we add anything else to our list?" I asked.

Someone in the back of the class said, "What about spelling and punctuation?" After a few ideas were tossed around, students wanted to assign a quantitative value to this criterion. It was agreed that there would be no more than five to seven spelling and mechanics errors allowed for a C.

As Mai was about to add this to the chart, Christine, who had been quiet throughout the discussion, presented a bit of logic that turned the issue of spelling and mechanics in a new direction. "This is a group project, not an individual student report," she said. "Wouldn't someone in the group probably find any spelling and punctuation errors? We should expect that there aren't *any* mistakes in a project like this." Almost everyone agreed at once with this idea.

Building on this idea, Kelley suggested, "Let's use that kind of rule for rubrics that just grade individual work." Everyone liked this idea, too, so with that issue resolved, we moved on to the B category.

How to Earn a B or an A

During my planning with Jane, she had suggested that each succeeding grade designation should include the criteria from the lower-grade categories, meaning that to get a B the student needed to have all the C criteria plus more. I shared this information with the class, and everyone agreed with this logic. So Mai made a large B on the chart paper and then wrote as the first entry, "All C criteria plus . . ."

I knew that this is where the real thinking would begin. The C category was predominately content descriptors, but now we needed quality descriptors.

"Okay, so what would a B poster need to have?" I asked. "What words or phrases can we think of to describe a better quality poster?"

Yohan called out, "How about four interesting facts?" Heads were nodding, so I knew the kids were equating *more* with *better.* Kids think in quantitative terms, so rather than expect a more sophisticated rubric during our first attempt, I built upon his idea.

As Mai wrote the phrase on the chart, I asked the class to look at each of the C descriptors and think about adding to or changing each one so that it reflected a better standard of quality. To keep everyone involved, I asked them to talk this over in their cooperative groups.

After a few minutes of active discussion, Raina suggested that the picture of the animal required for a C be a *colorful, detailed picture* for a B. I thought it sounded pretty good, and Mai was ready to write this down, when someone else blurted out, "No. That's too much for a B. I think that should be for an A."

Everyone started talking at this point. I learned that what sounded great to me was viewed quite differently by kids. In their minds, detail and color were two distinctly different attributes of quality. After a somewhat heated debate, this is how they resolved the issue: The B descriptor stated, "Colorful *or* detailed picture." The A descriptor would read, "Colorful *and* detailed picture."

The remaining descriptors were negotiated for the rest of the B and A categories. We kept to the order of criteria developed in the C category and just added the quality descriptors in sequence as we went through the B and A sections. Some criteria remained quantitative while others specifically stated the quality students wanted to see on the poster.

Student Ownership Through Active Participation

I allowed the kids to become as involved as possible throughout this entire process because I wanted them to have ownership in the rubric we created. I certainly could have ruled on many of the points of disagreement for them, but increasing student engagement was one of my major goals for this process. I could have short-circuited the debate to safeguard efficiency, but had I done so, I would have never achieved the kind of buy-in that I got. And because this was the first of many student-generated rubrics I would create with them, I wanted their first experience with this process to be one that hooked them.

Following is the finished version of that first rubric my class and I created.

Prehistoric Animal Poster Rubric (First Year)

C	B	A
• Large title and names of students • Description of animal • A picture • Diet and habitat • Two interesting facts • When and where the animal lived	All C criteria plus • Paragraph description of animal • Detailed or colorful picture • Four interesting facts	All B criteria plus • Colorful and detailed picture • Six or more interesting facts • May have extra picture • Labeled map may be included

Notice how the descriptors correlate to the focus questions. It is a very simple rubric, yet it's specific enough for students to know exactly how their posters will be evaluated. They understood it exactly because they were the ones who created it! One of the group posters produced for the unit is shown below.

First-Year Project

The Rubric Becomes the Road Map

After the rubric was created and posted in the classroom, students copied it for inclusion in their unit folders, chose an animal for their group to research, and organized themselves to begin work. I had made the announcement to students that although it was a group project and each member would share the group grade, each student was individually accountable for contributing to the overall project. "No hitchhiking on other people's brains," I warned them.

Students created fine posters even though I had no student work samples from a prior year to show them. What I learned from this process was that as students worked on their posters, they referred often to the rubric we had created, using it as a guide to resolve differences of opinion and to make decisions about what to include and what not to include. The rubric thus became a kind of road map, guiding them to their goal—a finished project that earned the grade they envisioned.

Second-Year Results

When I introduced this same unit the next year, my new students had the advantage of seeing samples of student projects from the previous year. As I showed my new class the focus questions for the prehistoric animal unit, the rubric created by the previous class, and the finished posters (I got to keep them!), the sixth-grade students saw how all the parts fit together.

When I introduced the rubric-writing activity, someone asked, "Why don't we just use the same rubric?" A few students readily agreed.

I explained that it was important for them to create their own rubric, to be an active part of determining how their work would be assessed so they would know exactly what each of the criteria meant.

"This won't be as clear to you unless you make your own rubric," I said. "We certainly can use last year's excellent rubric as a guide, but let's see whether we can improve it still further!"

With that challenge before them, the class began to work. As you compare the rubric that they created below with the rubric the first-year class created, I think you'll agree that they succeeded.

Prehistoric Animal Poster Rubric (Second Year)		
C	**B**	**A**
• Information is organized • Large title of animal • Description of animal • Animal's diet • Animal's habitat • Picture of animal	All C criteria plus • Neat and readable bold writing • Detailed description of animal • Two or more interesting facts • Colorful or detailed picture	All B criteria plus • Descriptive phrases in all areas of report • Four or more interesting facts • Colored and detailed illustrations • Labeled, colorful, realistic map with key • Writing that is as eye-catching as the drawings

Certain phrases from the second-year rubric still impress me. I was amazed when students came up with "neat and readable bold writing." We had been having a discussion about specificity and the goal of using accurate language that meant the same thing to everyone. As a class, we had discussed subjective terminology whenever an example of it arose so that we would share a common understanding of those terms.

For example, in responding to one student's suggestion to include the descriptor "writing shows effort and quality," I asked the class, "What does that mean to you? How can we say that in more specific terms?"

After asking them to clarify their thinking, I found that students became more specific. Words like *bold, neat,* and *readable* were suggested. Then Caylon put them all together and came up with "neat and readable bold writing." There was an almost tangible excitement over this phrase because everyone knew at once exactly what it meant.

Occasionally a phrase that made perfect sense to students seemed rather general to me, such as "descriptive phrases in all areas of report" or (in a later rubric) "all-round detail." But I always went with students' wording if I could see that it made perfect sense to them. I found this involvement absolutely critical to getting students to engage willingly in the entire process. This involvement made these rubrics truly student generated.

They say that a picture is worth a thousand words. That axiom certainly proved correct when I tried to convey the concept of content and quality work to my new students by showing them the prior year's rubric and work samples. The quality of the second-year project shown on the opposite page underscores how well they learned from the earlier samples.

I realized again that students want to do a good job and that they will meet teacher expectations if they understand clearly what is required. And that's what this model of assessment does: it takes the mystery out of grading in the minds of students.

Working Smarter

After we had completed a number of rubric-writing sessions during the first few months of the school year, I noticed that student participation had dropped off. Only a handful of students were coming up with the rubric descriptors. The rest of the class seemed willing to let a few kids do all the work. At the next opportunity, I shifted gears and announced, "Let's postpone until tomorrow the writing of our book-report rubric. For tonight's homework, I'd like each of you to write down the criteria for a C, B, and A that you think should be included in our rubric. Be prepared to share your ideas with the class tomorrow." Because students were quite familiar with the process we followed, I knew they could complete the assignment independently.

The next morning, every student in the class had a personal set of criteria ready to share. To facilitate this sharing of ideas, I broke students into teams and

Second-Year Project

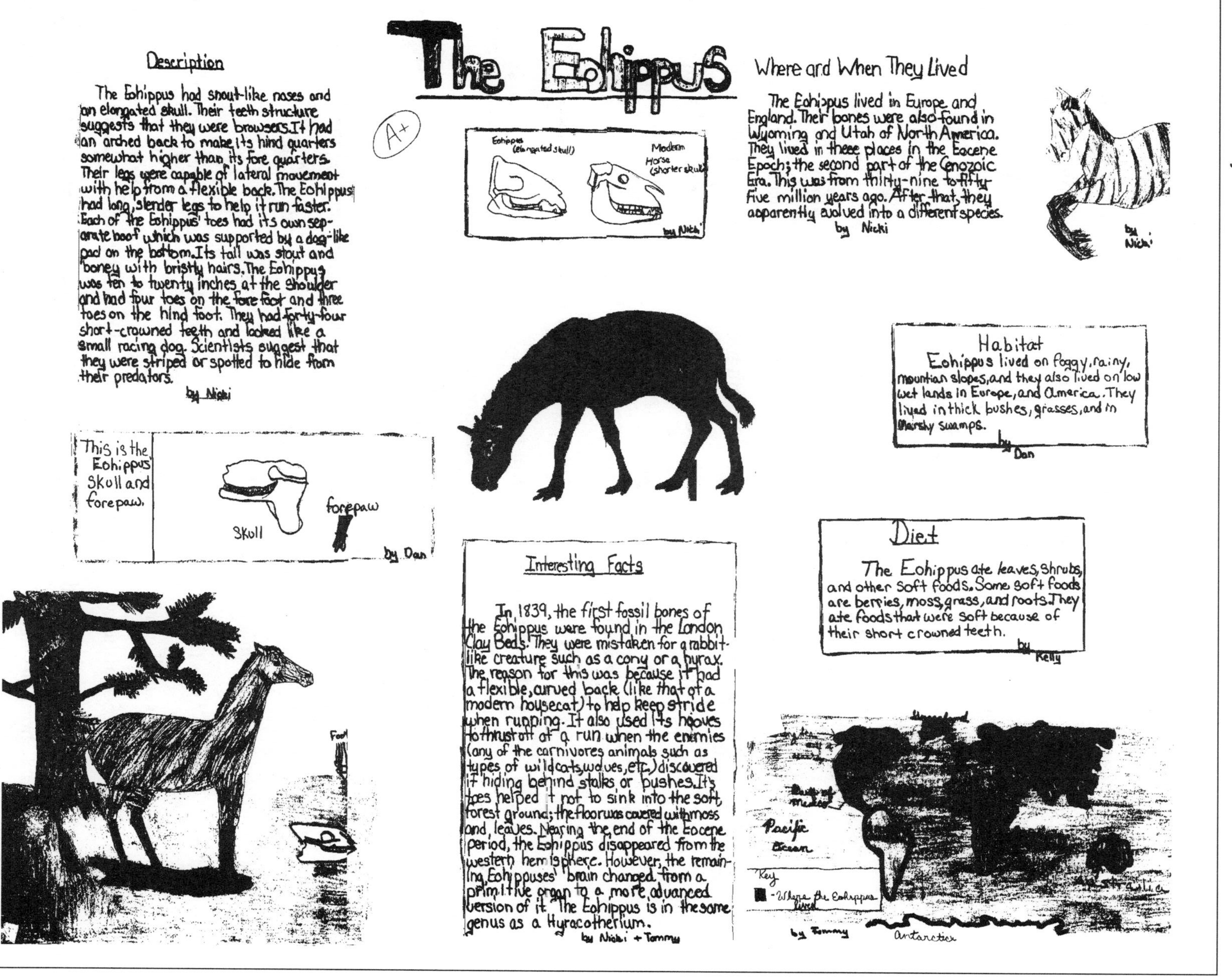

gave these instructions: choose a group recorder and take turns sharing your ideas for the C category.

I then announced, "Recorders, write down the ideas your team thinks are best for the C grade. Then repeat the process for both the B and A grades. When everyone is finished, you'll share your group's criteria with the rest of the class." Students quickly began working.

I was pleased by the level of engagement I found as I listened in on the conversations about why certain descriptor phrases or words should be included. Everyone was involved!

When all eight cooperative groups were finished, we had eight team rubrics. "Now what?" I thought. I was making this up as I went along.

"Good work, everyone," I said. "Now I need you to select a table representative who will take your team's rubric and bring it to the front of the room. These eight reps will continue working with the rubric and share the results with all of you in a little while." I asked the class to work on another assignment as I met privately with the eight group representatives.

I directed the eight students to do the following:

1. Break into two groups of four.
2. Choose a recorder for each group.
3. Exchange ideas from the rubrics created by the four teams represented in each group.
4. Have the recorder combine the best ideas contributed by the four teams.
5. Title the results "Best Ideas of Teams 1, 3, 5, and 7" and "Best Ideas of Teams 2, 4, 6, and 8."

After I made sure they all understood what I wanted, they went off in their two small groups and got to work.

Soon the two groups of students brought me the semifinalist rubrics representing the combined thinking of the entire class. I asked for two volunteers from among the eight representatives who would be willing to combine the two semifinalist rubrics into one "Best of Room 8" class rubric. They all knew this meant more thinking and did not jump to volunteer. I waited patiently. Finally two girls said, "Oh, give it to us. We'll do it." I thanked them generously. The other six students rejoined the class, and the girls began the process of combining the rubrics.

When they presented their handwritten rubric to me just before lunch, I realized with great satisfaction that the students truly understood the process we had been using for so many months. The two girls, however, were somewhat concerned. Their rubric was more detailed and specific than any we, as a class, had produced up to that point. The girls asked me whether it was too long. I answered, "Let's see what the rest of the class thinks."

During lunch, I made an overhead transparency of their handwritten rubric. As soon as the class returned from lunch recess, the girls placed the transparency on the overhead projector. I explained to the class what this transparency was and how the table representatives and the two girls had completed a rough draft combining the best student ideas.

"What we need to do now," I explained, "is review the rubric together and make any final revisions before we use it to complete your book-report assignment." I read each line aloud to the class and made the changes, deletions, and clarifications they suggested. At the conclusion of the revision process, I typed—from the heavily edited transparency—a final-draft version of the rubric and distributed a copy to each student. We were finished with what I felt was the first task-specific rubric totally authored by all students.

My Own Self-Reflection

As I reflected on this successful experience after school that day, I was very happy that I had discovered an innovative way to increase involvement by all students, both in the writing of the class-authored rubric and in its subsequent revision. I also made a mental note to myself for the next time we followed this process: I had led this discussion. What I should have done—especially since these were sixth graders now thoroughly familiar with the process—was to have the two girls who put it all together lead the class discussion. Thereafter, I did this with great success.

Reader's Assignment (Intermediate Teachers): Write a simple rubric with your students for the unit performance task you developed at the end of chapter 4.

7 Writing a Rubric in the Primary Classroom

Teachers who use rubrics at the primary level can focus on important areas other than grading. A student-generated rubric at this level gives teachers feedback on how well students follow directions while introducing students to self-evaluation and involving them in setting criteria for assessing their assignment.

In the last chapter, we observed a teacher training students to write a rubric. Now let's take a look at how Susan Chang, a kindergarten teacher, and Linda Spanier, a second-grade teacher, guided their students through the same process. (Notice that although the intermediate rubric began with C and built the rubric to an A, the primary teachers described in this chapter constructed their rubrics beginning with the top score. Both approaches are valid.)

Happy-Face Papers

Kindergarten teacher Susan Chang shared her story of introducing the use of rubrics to her young students.

"This morning I'm going to read you the story *Goldilocks and the Three Bears,*" I began. "After I read this story to you, I will ask you to draw three pictures: one picture for the beginning of the story, one picture for the middle of the story, and one picture for the end of the story. I would like you to use three colors in your drawings."

After I read the story to my students, I reviewed the task I wanted them to complete and drew a happy face on the chart paper. I told students, "We are now going to create a way of letting us know whether we've done a good job on our assignment. It is called a *rubric.*" I explained that the happy face meant a student followed directions. I wrote *followed directions* next to the happy face.

I then asked students, "If you do a good job, what should the three pictures look like? How can we tell whether a student followed directions?"

Katrina raised her hand. "The pictures should be about the story," she said. Martin added, "You need to have three pictures." I recorded both ideas on the chart.

Then I asked students, "How should the pictures be arranged?" After a few off-topic responses, Jerome raised his hand and said, "The pictures should be in the order of the story." I added that idea to the chart next to the happy face. Reuben added, "You have to use three colors in the pictures." I included this suggestion in the rubric.

Some students wanted to discuss which colors to use. Because this was our first rubric, I knew it was important to keep it as simple as possible. I told students, "You may make your own decision about which colors to use this time." Everyone smiled and nodded their heads.

Another student said, "It should be your best, neat work." All agreed that neatness was an important idea for the rubric. I added that descriptor to the chart. Though *best* and *neat* can be subjective terms, we discussed and agreed on the meaning of these words.

Straight-Face Papers

At this point I drew a straight face on the chart and explained, "A straight face means that a student didn't follow all the directions. What do you think a straight-face paper might look like?"

Nisha believed that a straight-face paper would be messy and only use one color. Other students suggested that the order of the pictures might be wrong or that they weren't about the story. I wrote both these excellent ideas on the chart under the straight face.

At the end of the discussion, I reviewed the criteria for a happy face and a straight face, posted the rubric in the classroom, and asked students to begin the assignment.

Below is the rubric the kindergarten class created along with one student's work.

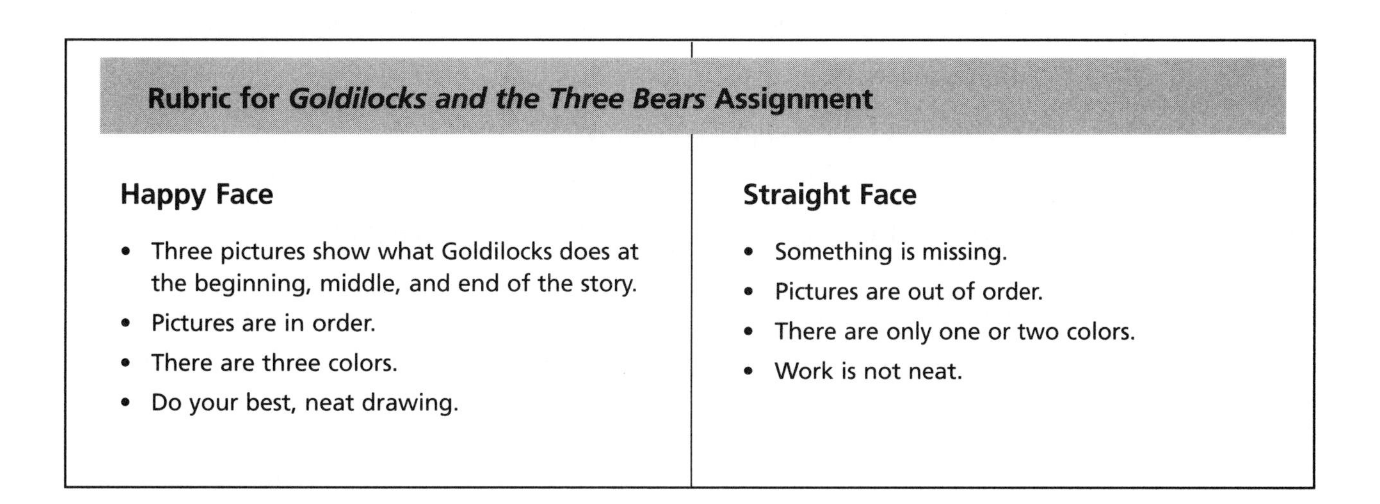

Rubric for *Goldilocks and the Three Bears* Assignment

Happy Face	Straight Face
• Three pictures show what Goldilocks does at the beginning, middle, and end of the story. • Pictures are in order. • There are three colors. • Do your best, neat drawing.	• Something is missing. • Pictures are out of order. • There are only one or two colors. • Work is not neat.

The next day, I asked for volunteers to stand up and share their finished work with the rest of the class. Then I explained how all students could decide how they did on the assignment by comparing their completed papers to the rubric (see chapter 10 for how we did this). I was happy to see that most of my students met the Happy Face criteria!

An Additional Step to Following Directions

You might want to consider adding another step to the process described above—a sample project. After giving directions to students and building the rubric together, do the following before students do their individual work:

1. Have students work in small groups to create a sample project that matches the directions for the assignment.
2. Ask groups to share their drawings with the entire class.
3. Lead students in a discussion about how the drawings match the rubric criteria.
4. Have students discuss how the drawings could be improved.

In this way, students will have a much clearer understanding of the assignment before they begin their individual drawings.

A Second-Grade Math Experience with Rubrics

Second-grade students typically spend much of their math time learning subtraction. Linda Spanier, a second-grade teacher eager to try a student-generated rubric in math, shared this story of her experience.

"My students had been using base-ten blocks to help them understand regrouping with ones, tens, and hundreds. One of the activities they participated in was a game called Ones, Tens, Hundreds. On the last day of the regrouping unit, I asked the children to explain their understanding of regrouping using words, pictures, and numbers. Following is a portion of the classroom discussion that led to the creation of the rubric we used to assess the activity."

I started by saying, "Today, we're going to make a 3-2-1 rubric for a math activity that you will be doing tomorrow. We have been using a rubric so far this year to grade our language practice each morning. Who would like to tell us something about that rubric?"

Several hands went up. I asked Carmen to tell us about a 3.

"You get a 3 if you have a complete sentence with a period at the end and a capital letter at the beginning," she said. "And you need to spell all the words in the sentence correctly."

"Jeff, can you tell us about a 2?" I asked.

"A 2 means you made a mistake. But you still have a capital letter and a period in your sentence," he answered.

"Sunjiah," I asked, "would you like to tell us about a 1?"

She replied, "A 1 means you made mistakes and you forgot the beginning capital letter and the period at the end."

To connect students' language-rubric experience with the task at hand, I said, "Now let's talk about what should be in a three-point math rubric. Think about the work we've done in math and how we might describe a good job." Then I had a wonderful idea! I glanced at Kian, our sixth-grade peer helper, standing quietly near the back of the room. "I know that Kian, who is here with us this morning, has had experience writing rubrics in her own class. Maybe, as we go along, she can give us some suggestions to help us write our math rubric."

Kian smiled as students turned to look at her. She said, "We have math rubrics in our class, and we spend a lot of time making sure everyone understands what the words in the rubric mean."

Jose, always ready to get started when I announce the next activity, put his hand up. "The 3 paper should have words, pictures, and numbers on it," he said. I was pleased to hear this because in recent weeks I had emphasized the use of words, pictures, and numbers to communicate understanding in our problem-solving activities. During our discussion about a 3, we decided that the words, pictures, and numbers on a student's paper needed to show that the student understood how ones, tens, and hundreds work together.

I then focused students' attention on the use of pictures. "What kind of pictures should be on a 3 paper?"

Students felt strongly that the pictures should relate to the math in the problem and not just to something added to the paper as a decoration. "Pictures must be about the math in the problem" is how students decided to phrase it.

I moved the discussion to the 2 category. "What would have to be missing from the 3 list for a paper to be a 2?" I asked.

Sam suggested the word *kinda* to show that a student had partial understanding of ones, tens, and hundreds. I asked students, "Do all of you understand *kinda*?" Everyone quickly said yes or nodded confidently.

At this point, Kian raised her hand. "Maybe it would be a good idea to have volunteers show what *kinda* means."

Several students immediately looked at me and waved their hands, hoping to be chosen. "Mona," I said, "can you go to the board and give us an example of what *kinda* means?"

Mona drew a picture to show how ones and tens are regrouped, but she did not show how tens and hundreds are regrouped. When she finished, many more hands wanted to draw their interpretations!

I allowed two other students to show their interpretation of *kinda*. After these examples were displayed, I could tell there was general understanding of the term. We then decided as a class to use *kinda* as a word that meant the student could have shown more understanding.

The finished 3-2-1 math rubric used to evaluate student understanding of the Ones, Tens, Hundreds game appears on the next page. Note how the order of each descriptor within a grade point remains the same in the other two grade categories. Kian suggested we follow this organizational idea as we wrote the rubric.

Ones, Tens, Hundreds Game Rubric		
3	**2**	**1**
• Has words, pictures, and numbers • Reader can understand how ones, tens, and hundreds work together • Pictures must be about the math in the problem	• Has words, pictures, and numbers • Reader can "kinda" understand how ones, tens, and hundreds work together • Pictures must be about the math in the problem	• Has words, pictures, and numbers • Reader cannot understand how ones, tens, and hundreds work together • Pictures are not about the math in the problem

Student Reaction

Linda's second-grade students were very excited to be involved in this process. It improved their understanding of the task and clarified the teacher's expectations for the assignment. Using the rubric to evaluate their own finished products (a process described in chapter 10) increased their enthusiasm for this method of assessment. Now that students completely understood what they needed to do to earn a 3 on their papers, most were able to produce work like the paper shown on the next page.

Although having the assistance of an older student was not essential, Kian's presence benefited students. It was clear to them that she understood the process they were engaged in. In addition, because she was from the upper grades, she served as an excellent ambassador for helping students realize that student-generated rubrics would be an ongoing component of their elementary-school experience.

Reader's Assignment (Primary Teachers): Write a simple rubric with your students for the performance task you selected in chapter 4.

11+11=22

Hundreds Tens 6+5=11 Ones 3

16
+16
32

+32
32
64

3+2=5

9+9=18

4+4=8 8+8=16

6+6=12

Charity Marino

The Ones, Tens and Hundreds

This is how you play the game. If you have more then 9 ones you have to put 10

Flat

Rod

Cube

dice

ones back. The you get a rode. If you get more the 9 10 you have to put all the 10 back. The you get a hundreds. If you run out of hundreds you use the tens. You don't throgh the dice. You use 2 dice.

use the tens. You don't throgh the dice. You use 2 dice.

8 Assessing Student Work: Peer Assessment and Self-Assessment

Just as it is important to involve students as much as possible in creating the rubric used to assess their completed performance task, it is equally important to involve them in the assessment process itself. There are three key reasons for this.

- *Student Motivation:* People naturally want to know how well they have performed on a given task. Students who evaluate their own work and the work of others using the assessment criteria that they helped create are more motivated to perform well.
- *Understanding Assessment Criteria:* By asking students to apply the assessment criteria they helped write, a standard for acceptable performance is established. Students internalize this standard and understand what the resulting grade means.
- *Reinforcement of Content:* During the assessment process, students are reviewing content related to the unit focus questions. Students are searching their performance-task projects to verify that they have the content required by the rubric, which continually reinforces their own understanding of the material presented.

If you have completed the reader's assignments given at the end of chapters 3 through 7, you have led your students in rubric writing *before* they worked on the performance task. Parents will also appreciate having the rubric before students begin work on a project; the rubric can guide parents as they help their children.

When your students have completed their projects, they are ready to assess their work. Have students attach a copy of the rubric to their own work, and then collect the papers and distribute them for peer assessment. The rubric should always travel with the work so that anyone looking at the work can see the criteria used to evaluate it. Parents especially appreciate this because it allows them to compare their child's work to the standards set on the rubric and therefore better understand the grade their child received.

The Grading Process We Follow

We have developed a list of steps—an overview of the assessment process used with student-generated rubrics—to guide our students through the assessment of their completed performance task. Each point will be illustrated with classroom examples in the next two chapters.

1. The teacher collects all student work and selects sample papers to use in a practice assessment session with the class.
2. The teacher reviews the rubric with students.
3. The teacher reads a sample paper aloud to the class.
4. Students identify rubric criteria contained in the sample paper.
5. The teacher and students discuss a grade based on the rubric for the sample paper.
6. Steps 3–5 are repeated several times to familiarize students with a wide range of work samples and to promote class agreement.
7. Students practice writing feedback comments on the grading form. (See page 107.)
8. The teacher assigns assessment partners.
9. Paper-flow procedures are explained to students.
10. The peer-assessment process takes place.
11. Papers are returned to their owners for self-assessment.
12. Students may appeal to challenge a grade.
13. The teacher reviews papers and makes final grade determinations.
14. Papers are returned to students for parent review and for inclusion in students' portfolios.

Thoughts to Consider

Keep the following thoughts in mind as you develop the assessment process.

- *Always partner students for peer assessment.* The discussion that takes place between two students keeps the process more objective and improves the accuracy of the grade. We want students to reach consensus within the assessment partnership, and this requires students to verify their decisions according to the rubric.
- *Grades and comments must be based on the rubric.* During the entire assessment process (peer, self, and teacher), it is important to emphasize that all comments must speak directly to the language in the rubric. Generalized comments like "Good job," or "You need to improve," or "Looks like you put a lot of effort into it" miss the point. The goal is to focus the assessment process on the specific performance descriptors. Comments based on the rubric improve self-evaluation by specifically identifying the work's weaknesses and strengths.
- *Preselect assessment partnerships.* When determining assessment partnerships, carefully consider who will work together effectively. Here are some suggestions for building partnerships.
  - — Match differing levels of ability. For example, partner more-capable students with those who may be struggling.
  - — Consider the needs of second-language learners and special-education students.
  - — Think about behavior combinations.
  - — Keep partnerships together long enough to establish good working relationships.
  - — Change partnerships periodically to promote interaction with other students.

Different Peer-Assessment Formats

Group projects and presentations can be assessed by small groups or the class as a whole.

- *Assessment in Cooperative Groups:* After a group presentation, the other cooperative teams discuss the presentation. Each group uses the rubric to reach consensus on a grade. The presenting group receives several grades (one from each of the other groups in the class) and one from the teacher. These can be averaged into a final grade for each of the team members. Involving more students in the project assessment greatly increases the validity of the grade.
- *Assessment as a Whole Class:* At the conclusion of the group's presentation, the teacher asks, "What comments—based on the rubric—can we make about this presentation?" The teacher then asks several students to share their own evaluations of the presentation. At the conclusion of this feedback session, each student in the class individually decides a grade, writes it on the assessment form, adds comments based on the rubric, signs the form, and delivers the grade card to the presenting group. To determine a final grade, individual scores from all students are averaged.

A Word About Individual Accountability

In our workshops, teachers often ask us how we justify giving a group grade to a member of the group who isn't participating and contributing fully to the group project. Our response to this is: We believe in protecting the rights of the other group members so that they may productively complete the assigned task. If a student chooses to not be a productive member of the group once the individual tasks within the group have been assigned, the teacher talks privately with the student and offers the choice of cooperating with the other group members or doing the project individually. In our experience, students usually decided to remain in the group and to contribute.

Individual accountability also means each student must demonstrate that he or she has learned the subject matter. At the conclusion of a group project, we ask all students to answer the focus questions in writing. We then assign a grade to these individual student responses based on teacher judgment of how thoroughly the students answered the questions.

Reader's Assignment: Assess several papers by yourself (or with a grade-level team member) using the rubric you developed with your students in chapter 6 (intermediate) or chapter 7 (primary).

9 Teaching Intermediate Students to Assess

Getting students involved in the assessment process begins with including them in rubric writing. Students then assess the tasks and further increase their ownership in the process. In this chapter, we return to the authors' classrooms—first to Larry Ainsworth's sixth-grade class and later to Jan Christinson's fifth-grade class—to observe intermediate students learning to assess their own and others' completed performance tasks.

Larry's Class: Proactive Assessment

Katie brought her completed science-fiction-book mobile to school the first day back from the two-week winter vacation, several days before the performance task was due. Other students looked at each other, wondering whether they had missed an important deadline, and Katie looked at the class and wondered why she was the only one holding a completed project! I was inspired.

"Katie," I asked, "since you brought your mobile in early, would you be willing to let the class assess your performance task according to our rubric?" Katie agreed. The other students, greatly relieved to find out that their work was not yet due, eagerly carried out my next request. I instructed them to look closely at Katie's mobile for evidence that all rubric criteria were present.

During the next 30 minutes, I read each line of the rubric aloud to the class as Katie scanned her project to verify the presence of that criterion and showed it to the class. Students paid close attention as we looked for evidence of whether Katie had included all required criteria. By the time we finished, Katie and the class agreed that her present project would receive a B.

At that point, I asked Katie whether she knew what was missing from her work. Using the rubric criteria, Katie and the class together were able to identify the specific improvements she needed to boost her final grade to an A. By analyzing Katie's mobile against the rubric, every student now knew exactly what those rubric descriptors meant in terms of an actual finished product.

The result? On the actual day the mobiles were due, my students all walked in with wonderful projects, most of which earned the coveted grade of A. I am happy to report that Katie's was among them! The class applauded Katie's grade, and I thanked her again for allowing us to evaluate her work in front of everyone. It had helped all students succeed.

As I realized the full impact of how comparing Katie's work to the student-generated rubric had clarified the performance expectations for my students, I marveled at the power of this model of assessment. The experience proved to be one of the most pivotal half hours of the entire academic year.

Preparing Sixth Graders to Assess

In our classroom, we had been doing a math Problem of the Week every week, but were having trouble deciding how to assess the work. My students and I decided to write a Problem of the Week Rubric. This rubric was different from all the others we had created in that its specific descriptors could be applied to any Problem of the Week students solved, not just one. This general Problem of the Week Rubric—based on the Problem of the Week Guide I created—was necessary because it would take too much time to create a separate math rubric each week. (Blackline masters for these can be found on pages 108 and 109.)

To begin the Problem of the Week assessment process, I ask student volunteers to show how they solved the problem and to explain their process to the class. (Whenever students solve word problems, I always direct them to show their work by using words, pictures, and numbers. This generally results in a complete demonstration of students' understanding of the problem.) Other students can ask for clarification or add their own suggestions to further clarify the solution. Once everyone completely understands the correct solution, we review the rubric together.

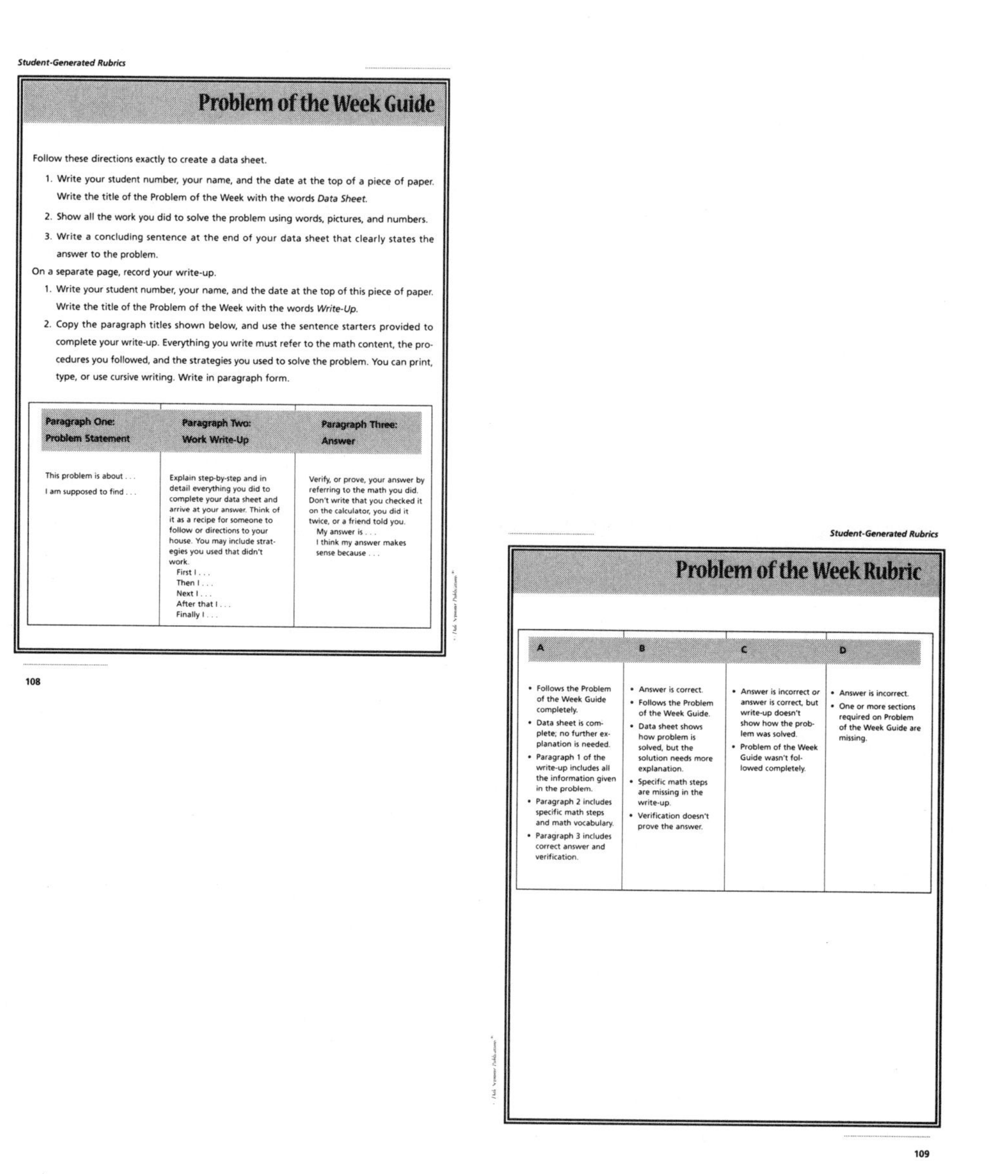

Problem of the Week Guide

Follow these directions exactly to create a data sheet.

1. Write your student number, your name, and the date at the top of a piece of paper. Write the title of the Problem of the Week with the words *Data Sheet*.
2. Show all the work you did to solve the problem using words, pictures, and numbers.
3. Write a concluding sentence at the end of your data sheet that clearly states the answer to the problem.

On a separate page, record your write-up.

1. Write your student number, your name, and the date at the top of this piece of paper. Write the title of the Problem of the Week with the words *Write-Up*.
2. Copy the paragraph titles shown below, and use the sentence starters provided to complete your write-up. Everything you write must refer to the math content, the procedures you followed, and the strategies you used to solve the problem. You can print, type, or use cursive writing. Write in paragraph form.

Paragraph One: Problem Statement	Paragraph Two: Work Write-Up	Paragraph Three: Answer
This problem is about . . . I am supposed to find . . .	Explain step-by-step and in detail everything you did to complete your data sheet and arrive at your answer. Think of it as a recipe for someone to follow or directions to your house. You may include strategies you used that didn't work. First I . . . Then I . . . Next I . . . After that I . . . Finally I . . .	Verify, or prove, your answer by referring to the math you did. Don't write that you checked it on the calculator, you did it twice, or a friend told you. My answer is . . . I think my answer makes sense because . . .

Problem of the Week Rubric

A	B	C	D
• Follows the Problem of the Week Guide completely. • Data sheet is complete; no further explanation is needed. • Paragraph 1 of the write-up includes all the information given in the problem. • Paragraph 2 includes specific math steps and math vocabulary. • Paragraph 3 includes correct answer and verification.	• Answer is correct. • Follows the Problem of the Week Guide. • Data sheet shows how problem is solved, but the solution needs more explanation. • Specific math steps are missing in the write-up. • Verification doesn't prove the answer.	• Answer is incorrect or answer is correct, but write-up doesn't show how the problem was solved. • Problem of the Week Guide wasn't followed completely.	• Answer is incorrect. • One or more sections required on Problem of the Week Guide are missing.

The rubric and a grading form (see page 107) are then stapled on top of the completed work write-up. I collect all papers and distribute half of them to the peer-assessment teams, which have two members each.

The first step in teaching students to peer assess is to *anchor* the class: provide benchmark papers so students can see what an A paper contains in terms of content and quality, what a B paper contains, and so on. Students must be taught how to look at other students' papers and find elements required by the rubric.

Sometimes I show students anchor papers I have identified. Other times I ask the class, "Who thinks they have an A paper?" A student will then read the paper aloud and explain why that paper is an A, based on the rubric. I will ask for other papers to be read until I sense that the class as a whole understands how to identify an A, B, and C paper. When everyone can use the rubric to identify the correct grade, I know students are anchored and ready to begin the actual peer-assessment process.

I direct students to read through the entire paper first to familiarize themselves with its content. Then, using the rubric, partners look for evidence of the specific criteria, checking off the appropriate boxes on the rubric as that evidence is found. Once this procedure is complete, partners can determine the grade based on the degree to which the rubric criteria have been met for each grade category. They then write the grade under Peer Grade, add comments (under Justification), and show those comments to the teacher, who verifies that the comments are appropriate (that is, related to rubric criteria).

When the peer-assessment stage is completed, the teacher distributes the papers to their owners for self-grading and possible appeal. Papers are then returned to the teacher for final grading and comments. Once the grading criteria on a rubric have been checked, the grading comments may look like this.

Peer graders Michael R **and** Danny

Grade A **Justification** all "A" Critera

Self-grade A **Justification** all "A" criteria

Teacher's grade (A) **Comments** I agree. All "A" criteria included.

Appropriate comments made by grading partners are not compliments. The purpose of the comments is to give students constructive feedback. For example, if partners decide the paper is a B, they must write a comment based on the rubric that clearly specifies what's missing—what kept that paper from being graded an A. Here is an example of the comments for the Problem of the Week reproduced in chapter 15 (see page 100).

Peer graders Megan **and** Clair

Grade B Justification Verification doesn't prove answer.

Self-grade B Justification verification did not prove my answer

Teacher's grade (B) Comments I agree. You had all "B" criteria, but not all "A" criteria

Students need to practice writing appropriate and helpful comments before actually grading their own and other's completed performance tasks. Since the grading comments may eventually become part of the portfolio selections reviewed during parent conferences, it's important to set acceptable standards with students and maintain those standards throughout the year.

Monitoring Students as They Do Peer Assessment

Students continually discuss the content as they complete a peer assessment. Often they bring a particular paper to me, either for clarification or to ask my opinion on a particular section of the write-up. I try to help them make the decision rather than making it for them, and the rubric always serves as our guide. I ask the peer assessors to look for proof that the student fulfilled each criterion in the rubric. Sometimes partners cannot see whether the student addressed a specific issue, and at those times, I review the paper and resolve the issue with the students.

It is important to monitor students as they do peer assessment, not only for you as the teacher, but also for other students. You can listen in on the discussions students are having as they assess other students' work and gain insight into individual student understanding. I have often interrupted a session to clarify an important point for the entire class after I observed student partnerships having difficulty assessing a particular section. These interruptions are actually teachable moments in which everyone's understanding is advanced.

Self-Assessment

Just as peer-grading partners must follow the rubric when determining a grade, individual students must base their self-assessments on the rubric. Occasionally a student will feel unfairly graded and will want to appeal the grade. Reasons for this vary, but usually they stem from the amount of effort put into the task—the assumption being that this effort ought to guarantee a higher grade. This is where the comments written by the partners become decidedly important. Because the comments must be specific and address the missing content or quality according to the rubric descriptors, students who appeal should understand clearly what was lacking in their work and thus why they received the given grade.

On the other hand, if a student has been unfairly assessed and the comments do not justify the grade or they can be refuted, the teacher can resolve the issue fairly in a conference with the grading partners and the student. When the teacher monitors the grading process, students can be actively involved in using the rubric they created to assess the paper while still benefiting from the teacher's direct supervision. An example of this can be seen in the comments on the grading form shown below. The peer graders thought Justin's data sheet needed further explanation. Justin thought it did not and appealed in writing his grade on the self-grade portion of the rubric. I reviewed the paper and explained to all three students that the data sheet sufficiently proved his correct answer. Everyone was satisfied.

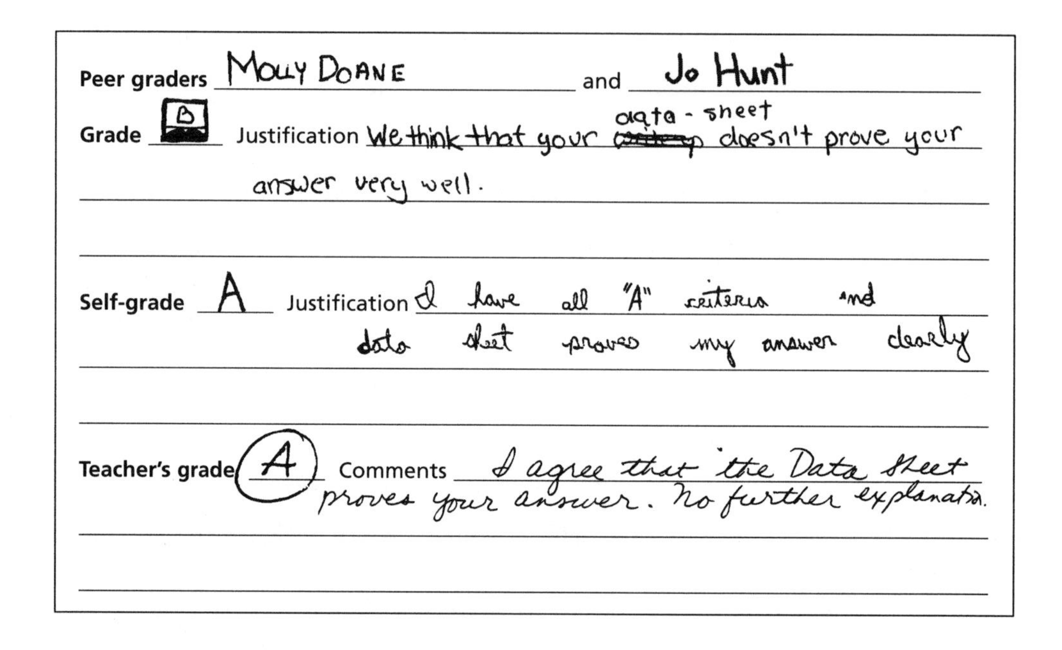

Peer graders MOLLY DOANE and Jo Hunt

Grade B Justification We think that your data-sheet doesn't prove your answer very well.

Self-grade A Justification I have all "A" criteria and data sheet proves my answer clearly

Teacher's grade A Comments I agree that the Data Sheet proves your answer. No further explanation.

Teacher Has the Final Say

The last step in the assessment process is the teacher's assessment of student work. Students should understand from the beginning that the final decision always rests with the teacher. It is also important to make this point when sharing this assessment method with parents during back-to-school night or parent conferences. Because students have been actively involved throughout the grading process, they understand the grades given by the teacher.

Jan's Class: Training Fifth Graders to Assess

In my fifth-grade classroom, students completed a social-studies unit on the original 13 colonies. These were the unit focus questions.

1. Where were the colonies located?
2. Who settled each region of colonization?
3. Why did people come to each region?
4. How did people live in each region?

Students knew from the beginning of the unit that their performance task would be to write a five-paragraph essay about the colonization of three different regions. These were my directions to them: "You are to write a separate paragraph about the colonization of each area. Each paragraph must answer the focus questions for that region. In other words, your paragraph on the southern colonies must answer all four focus questions. Then you will answer all four focus questions for the middle colonies in the second paragraph and all four for the New England colonies in the third paragraph."

Before students began writing, we reviewed the colony essay rubric that the class had already created. Notice that the rubric descriptors address completeness of content as opposed to quality of writing.

Colony Essay Rubric

A	B	C
• All focus questions answered for each colonial region • Five-paragraph style complete (introduction, body, conclusion) • Readable cursive writing • Correct information • Minor or no information missing (*minor* understood by class)	• One or two focus questions total not answered (incorrect information or answer not included) • Five-paragraph style complete • Readable cursive writing	• Three or more focus questions not answered (incorrect or not included) • Five-paragraph style complete • Readable cursive writing

Assessing Essays: A Two-Step Process

I have found that when the performance task is an essay, assessment is a two-step process: First a pair of students reads the essay looking for the answers to the focus questions. During the second reading, a second pair of grading partners determines the grade based on the rubric.

The day after students turned in their essays, I gave them these instructions.

1. Gather all your study notes and information pertaining to the colonies.
2. Individually review your study materials to refamiliarize yourselves with the content.
3. Move into your assigned partnerships.
4. Review with me the rubric and the focus questions.

To anchor the class, I instructed students to listen carefully and refer to their study charts as I read aloud the paragraph about the southern colonies from a preselected student essay. I challenged the class to see whether that student had answered the four focus questions within the paragraph.

"How many agree that the first focus question was answered in the paragraph?" I asked. A majority of hands went up. I then asked whether anyone disagreed.

Ahmed raised his hand and said, "I don't think it said where the colonies were located." Students listened as I read the paragraph again.

D'Lisa raised her hand. "No," she said, "the location is mentioned." Heads nodded, and Ahmed realized he had not been listening carefully enough.

I then read aloud the paragraph about the middle colonies and asked, "Did you hear answers to all four focus questions? Was any information about the middle colonies left out?"

Tsung answered, "I noticed nothing was said about all the different groups that settled the middle colonies." Other students agreed that Tsung was correct.

I replied, "Yes, this writer mentioned two groups that settled the area but not all the others. So the second focus question was not answered completely."

I repeated this process for the paragraph about the New England colonial region, again emphasizing the identification of the content that specifically addressed the focus questions.

Assessing Content

When I felt confident that students could compare each paragraph to the rubric independently, I passed out the essays and directed partners to sign their names at the end of the papers and read the papers for content. Then I directed them to place numbers 1 to 4 in the margin by each paragraph. The four numbers corresponded to the four focus questions. Students indicated whether the necessary content was present or missing by writing a plus or minus next to each number. An example is shown on the next page.

As partners finished grading the paper for content, they brought it to me for a quick review. I asked them whether they had any concerns about the assessment. If they did, we discussed them immediately and reached a decision.

Students knew that I was available to provide clarification as needed. Monitoring the assessment and resolving uncertainties during the process and not *after* the grading was very important. In addition, the teacher needs to hear student discussions, read their comments, and be actively involved in training students to use a rubric.

When a partnership completed one paper, they turned the paper in to me, and I gave them a second paper. Once all papers had been assessed for content, we were ready to move to grading.

A different pair of students then read an essay to briefly check the content and assess the overall quality based on the rubric descriptors. They wrote the grade and their comments on the assessment form and signed it. They brought the paper to me, and I checked the accuracy of their comments and grade decision. I again asked them whether they had any concerns about the paper. If peer assessors did not follow directions and were not accurate in their assessment, I wouldn't accept the paper until they made the needed corrections. Students then

5 paragraph complete

Kris
2/14/95

Colony test

The colonization of America by European countries happend in 3 diffrent eras. The 13 colonies developed in the Southern, Middle, and the New England areas of the Atlantic Coast.

The Southern Colonies are located South of floridia and North of Maryland. The main people that settled the southern colonies were investors, slaves, indentured servonts, men and Boys. Investors came to profit the New World. Slaves came from Africa unwillingley. Indentured servants came because if they worked for 5 years they would get 100 acers of land, food, and clothing. They lived off of cash crops, small farms, New England trading route.

1 −
2 ±
3 ±
4 ±

Plantations

The Middle Colonies are South of New York and North of Delaware. The Colonies are New york, Delaware, Pensylvania, and new Jersey. The people that settled the Middle colonies were English, Irish, Dutch, france, Welsh, scots, Sweeds. They came for religous freedom and farms. They lived off of rich ferdel soil, big water supplies, farms.

1 −
2 +
3 +
4 −

How did they live?

The New England Colonies are South of New Hampshire and North of Connecticut. The Colonies are New Harapshire, Massachusetts, Rhode island, Connecticut. The people that settled the New england Colonies were the Purilins from England. The Puritins came for a new a life and for religious belifs. They lived on a trading route. The trading route was that they would buy an item and sell it for more. So they would get profits.

1 −
2 +
3 +
4 +

merchants

In Conclusion, the original 13 colonies developed in 3 major areas in several diffrent ways.

C/B
Brian Berson
Kimberly

placed the paper on the "graded" pile, took another paper from the "ungraded" pile, and began the process again. This process we refer to as *paper-flow procedures.*

In this procedure, when all the papers are graded, they are returned to their owners for self-assessment and possible appeal. If a student feels unfairly graded, an appeal in writing with specific references to the rubric may be submitted to me. I require students to submit a written appeal rather than an oral one so there is a written record of the appeal that refers to the rubric. In most cases, the self-assessment matches the peer grader's assessment.

Teaching students to evaluate their own work and the work of others using a set of criteria they themselves created is the heart of this assessment model. Even though it takes time to teach students the steps in the process, that time is well spent. As the year progresses, students become increasingly comfortable with the process and respect the validity of the grades they receive. Teacher monitoring of student-assessment decisions—which at first is extensive—decreases as students become more adept at determining the relationship between the rubric and the actual work produced.

Reader's Assignment: Try the peer-assessment process with your students using the finished performance tasks.

10 Teaching Primary Students to Assess

Although most primary students are not ready for peer assessment, they are quite capable of self-assessment. They benefit from self-assessment in two ways.

- Students understand the expectations of the classroom environment.
- Students learn to determine how well they have followed directions.

First-grade teachers have successfully used rubrics to help students understand how they are expected to behave in the classroom. For example, first graders can assist the teacher in developing a rubric that describes appropriate behavior for students engaged in learning-center activities. The teacher can periodically ask students to stop their activity momentarily and evaluate their own behavior based on the rubric. This process of comparing present behavior to a classroom standard encourages students to become more responsible for their own behavior.

Primary students are also able to compare their own work to a simple rubric created in the classroom to determine whether they have followed directions. To see how this self-assessment takes place in the kindergarten classroom, let us revisit the students from chapter 7 and note how teacher Susan Chang guides them through this self-assessment process.

Self-Assessment and a Plan for Improvement

"Remember the three drawings you made about *Goldilocks and the Three Bears*?" I began. "Today we're going find out how well you followed directions. Let's look at the rubric we wrote together yesterday."

I directed everyone's attention to the rubric and returned the papers to their authors. Then I read aloud the first line of the rubric and said, "Look at your paper and count to see whether you have three pictures. Raise your hand if you have all three." All hands went up! With pride in my voice, I announced, "It looks like everyone followed the first direction."

I continued, "Now look to see whether your pictures are in order. Is your first picture from the beginning of the story? Is your second picture from the middle of the story? Is your last picture from the end of the story? If you're not sure about one of your pictures, please raise your hand."

After helping a few students, I asked the class, "Now please raise your hand if your pictures are in order." Most of the children raised their hands.

Now I asked them, "Did you remember to use three or more colors?" I observed students counting the colors in their drawings. Most discovered that they had followed that direction, too.

The final item on the rubric addresses neatness, so I asked students, "Please decide whether you think this is your neatest work." I waited a moment as everyone thought about this.

"Now pick up your crayon. Did you answer yes to all my questions about your paper? If you did, please draw a happy face on your paper now. If you forgot something, please draw a straight face now." Students did this, and almost immediately several wanted to share their self-assessments.

Maria said, "I gave myself a happy face because I did everything that was on the rubric." Billy wanted to share next. "I only used two colors in my picture, so I gave myself a straight face." Several others shared with the class.

The last thing I had students do was talk with a classmate about how they could do a better job next time. This final step of having students make a simple plan for improvement and tell their plan to another student is important because it increases students' personal responsibility for their own learning.

As I listened to students talk together, I noted that most did understand what they had done correctly in their work and what they would do differently next time. They really enjoyed putting those happy faces on their own papers, too!

I knew that the few students who would receive a straight face needed more guidance with the assignment requirements so they could be equally successful.

I decided to meet with those students and offer them the chance to redo their pictures after helping them identify the improvement needed. I knew this would give them valuable feedback in following directions.

Anchoring Primary Students

When second-grade teacher Linda Spanier was ready to lead her students through the assessment of the Ones, Tens, Hundreds Game described in chapter 7, she began by selecting sample papers and reviewing the rubric with students. Here is her description of that part of the assessment process.

"Boys and girls," I said, "today we're going to use the rubric we made to grade our math papers. The most important part of the rubric is whether your paper shows how ones, tens, and hundreds work together. I want you to listen carefully for this information as I read a few papers. Then I want you to decide whether each paper is a 3, 2, or 1."

I held up the first paper and read it to the class. Then I asked, "How many of you think this is a 3?" Several hands went up. "Keung," I asked, "would you tell us why you think it's a 3?" He replied, "When I listened to you read the paper, I could tell the person understood how ones, tens, and hundreds work together." Other students' comments supported Keung's opinion.

I read another paper. This time it was obvious to students that something was missing. Akayla said, "I think this is a 2 because I can understand how ones and tens go together but not tens and hundreds."

I continued this process until I felt students were comfortable with the distinctions between a 3, 2, and 1. I knew they were now anchored and ready to try assessing their own work. As I later reviewed the papers, I was pleased to see that for the most part, students' self-assessments matched my own assessment of their level of understanding.

Peer Assessment in Primary Grades

Upper-primary students may be ready to move beyond self-assessment and experiment with peer assessment. Those with a lot of experience judging their own work against rubrics are ready to learn how to assess their peers. We have seen third graders transition from self-assessment to peer assessment quite effectively.

To help students succeed in peer assessment, follow these guidelines.

- Choose a simple task that does not require in-depth content.
- Use a three-point rubric: 1, 2, 3 or A, B, C.
- Include items in the rubric that can be counted by students.
- Keep the rubric simple: use specific language, not subjective terms open to interpretation.

Third Graders Use a Rubric as a Checklist for Content

Third-grade social-studies curriculum often focuses on the community in which students live. Third-grade teacher Kelley Ebel introduced her students to peer assessment using this student-created rubric for a travel brochure that included a picture and description of the land, plants, animals, and climate of their city.

Travel Brochure Rubric		
1	**2**	**3**
• Title • Student names • Four pictures • At least one sentence included in each description (land, plants, animals, climate) • Map on front	All 1 criteria plus • Four detailed pictures • At least two sentences included in each description • Neatness • Detailed map	All 2 criteria plus • Three or more sentences in each description • Colorful, detailed map • Big, bold title

Kelley placed students in peer-assessment partnerships. Knowing that her students would succeed in evaluating their peers' work if they limited their grading to the identification of content only, she gave each pair of students a travel brochure like the one shown on the opposite page and a copy of the rubric, instructing them to use it as a checklist.

"Since this is our first time grading with a partner," I said, "we're going to do this all together. Let's look at the first phrase in the 1 section of the rubric. Now look at the travel brochure in front of you, and find the title. If the brochure has a title, put a star in the box in front of the first line of the rubric. If it doesn't have a title, put a check mark in the box in front of the first line of the rubric."

Students did as they were directed. I had them repeat this process for each line of the rubric, moving from the 1 category into the 2 and ending with the 3. After this, I passed out the assessment form and instructed students to discuss with their partners what the grade should be based on their stars and check marks. "You and your partner talk it over, make a decision about the grade, and write it on the form at the bottom of the rubric paper."

When everyone was finished, I asked whether any students wanted to share with the class the grade they had given the brochure and the reasons for doing so.

Romela said, "Sarah and I gave this brochure a 2 because it has only two sentences and it needs three."

"Good job," I replied. "The reasons you gave are the kind of comments I want you to write on the grading form."

I then instructed students to talk with their partners and decide what comments to write. "If you put a star in front of each line of the entire rubric," I said, "write 'You followed all the directions.'" I reminded them that if the grade was not a 3, their comments must tell what was missing.

After all papers were graded, I returned them to the owners for self-assessment. "Now I'd like you to grade your own travel brochure the same way you graded your classmate's brochure," I told them. "Remember to write down your grade and the reasons you think you deserve this grade."

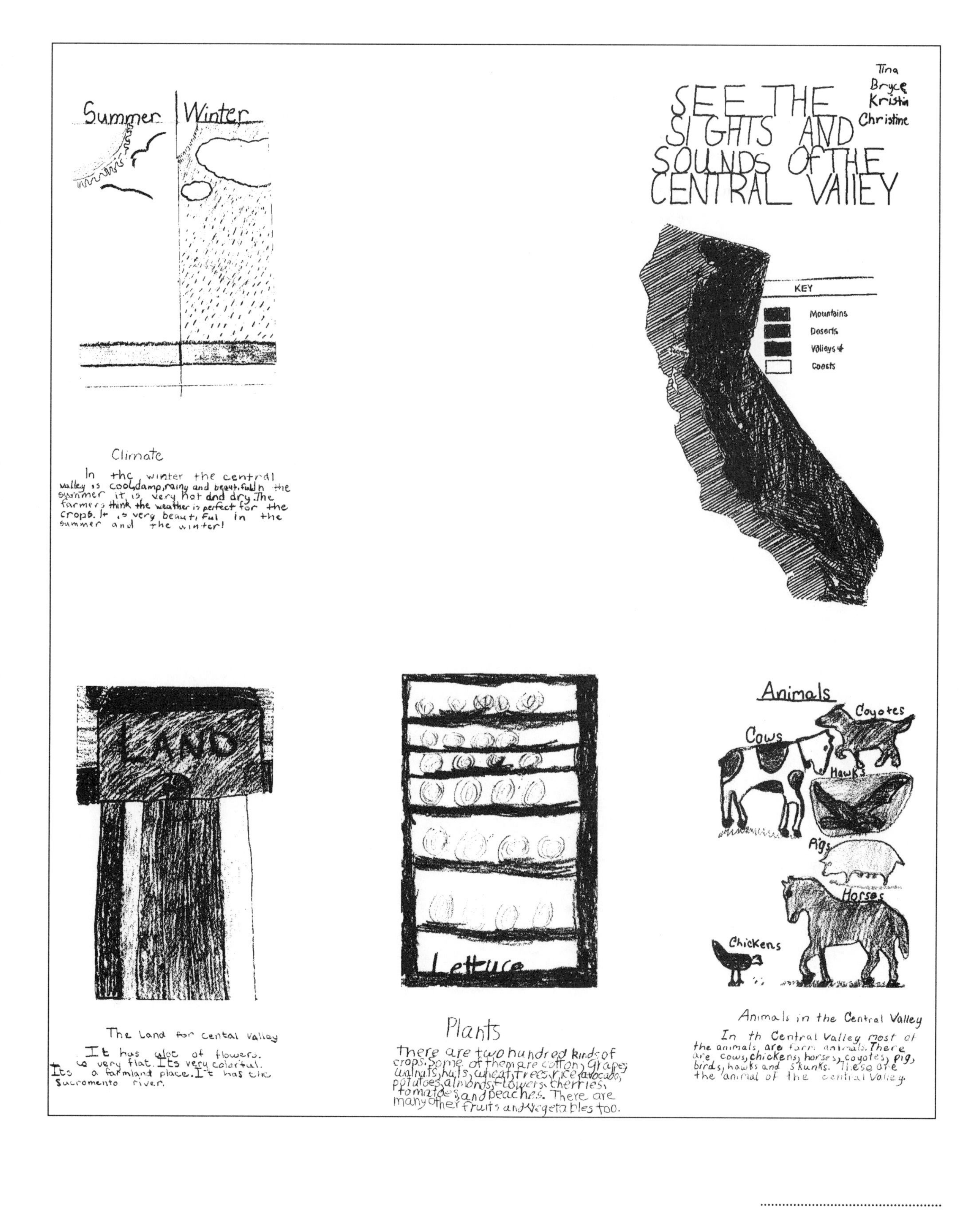

Tina
Bryce
Kristin
Christine
SEE THE SIGHTS AND SOUNDS OF THE CENTRAL VALLEY
Summer
Winter
KEY
Mountains
Deserts
Valleys
Coasts
Climate
In thc winter the central valley is cool,damp,rainy and beautiful.In the summer it is very hot and dry.The farmers think the weather is perfect for the crops. It is very beautiful in the summer and the winter!
LAND
Lettuce
Animals
Coyotes
Cows
Hawks
Pigs
Horses
Chickens
The Land for cental valley
It has aloc of flowers. is very flat. Its very colorful. Its a farmland place. It has the Sacromento river.
Plants
there are two hundred kinds of crops. Some of them are cotton, Grapes, walnuts, nuts, wheat, trees, rice, avocado, potatoes, almonds, flowers, cherries, tomatoes, and peaches. There are many other fruits and vegetables too.
Animals in the Central Valley
In th Central Valley most of the animals are farm animals. There are cows, chickens, horses, coyotes, pig, birds, hawks and skunks. These are the animal of the central Valley.

When I later reviewed the peer assessments and the self-assessments, I evaluated how well students had used the rubric to determine each grade. I was thrilled that the majority of comments showed that they had listened to my directions. In most instances, my own assessment of their work matched the grades students had given.

Reader's Assignment: Have your students self-assess their completed performance tasks, using the rubric you created together.

The Final Steps: From Self-Reflection to Parent Conference

In her article "The Horse Before the Cart: Assessing for Understanding" (*Educational Leadership* [February 1994]: 22–23), Rebecca Simmons writes, "Taking time and energy to reflect on and improve one's work are essential to the understanding process itself."

As we've stated, the goals of this assessment model are to fully involve students in the evaluation process and to teach them to discern their own degree of understanding. Asking students to reflect on their own participation during the unit makes their learning more meaningful: "Self-evaluation promotes metacognition skills, ownership of learning, and independence of thought. The ability to assess one's own progress is powerful" (Jean Kerr Stenmark, ed., *Mathematics Assessment: Myths, Models, Good Questions, and Practical Suggestions,* [Reston, Va.: National Council of Teachers of Mathematics, 1991], 55).

Student Self-Reflection

The sole purpose of self-reflection should be to improve performance in subsequent assessments and beyond. "Self-assessment . . . will promote learning. Students who think about and discuss their progress toward the achievement of class goals . . . on the basis of the evidence they see in their own work, will build better understanding and control of their own success" (ibid., 56).

We have our students engage in self-reflection at the conclusion of each unit of study. The purpose for this is twofold.

- to evaluate their own task performance related to the specific learning outcomes of the unit
- to develop a plan for improvement in subsequent units and similar assessment projects

In teaching students to self-reflect, the emphasis should be on helping them identify the elements of their actual performance ("I answered each of the focus questions") and not merely on the sharing of subjective opinions about their performance ("I know I did a good job because I tried hard").

Following is a sample of the self-reflection format we use with students at the conclusion of a major unit. A blackline master for this can be found on page 106.

Student-Generated Rubrics

Name ______________________ Date ________

Self-Reflection Form

1. How well did you learn the information necessary to answer the focus questions for this unit? Explain.

2. Discuss how you did on the performance task for this unit. What are you pleased with? What could you have done better?

3. What is your specific plan for improvement? What will you do differently next time?

Here is how one fifth-grade student answered the self-reflection questions following his performance on the five-paragraph colonization essay. Try to distinguish his subjective opinions from his actual performance.

Answer to Question 1: I forgot to include the information about plantations in the southern colonies, but I knew everything else.

Answer to Question 2: I did a great job on the five-paragraph essay form.

Answer to Question 3: My plan is to try harder and ask my parents for help.

This student shows progress toward writing specific remarks on his performance in the first response, but he did not answer both parts of question two. Notice, too, that the word *great* is subjective. The third response is quite typical of a student's early attempts at self-reflection: the plan does not clearly spell out what the student will do to improve.

Here is another set of sample responses. These statements could be a model for other students; they answer all the questions and provide a very specific plan for improvement.

Answer to Question 1: I was able to answer all three questions about the colonies, but I left out the information for question number four in the paragraphs on southern and middle colonies.

Answer to Question 2: I was happy that I put in all the parts of the five-paragraph essay and that I remembered how to do the introductory paragraph. I need to do a better job on the concluding paragraph. I said the same things in both the first and last paragraphs instead of restating the information like I was supposed to.

Answer to Question 3: My plan is to give myself more time to learn all the information and to practice writing the essay two times at home. I also need to look at the rubric better before I take the test so I put in the right things.

Because students usually do not know how to write a thoughtful self-reflection, we use these steps to train them.

1. As a class, students discuss and clarify the three questions together.
2. Students write their initial responses.
3. The teacher asks for volunteers to share their self-evaluations aloud.

   (Often students are rather self-conscious about sharing their thoughts with the class, but there are always a few who are willing to do so. These students become excellent role models, providing insightful, well-written responses for other students to emulate. This sharing of responses becomes an important springboard for a class discussion aimed at improving students' ability to write appropriate self-reflections.)
4. Students work with partners, sharing their own responses and exchanging feedback.

5. Students revise their own self-reflections to include comments more specific to their actual performance.

Teacher Self-Reflection

A major benefit to eliciting this kind of feedback from students is that it enables the teacher to gain insights into the effectiveness of the instruction and of the performance task itself. Questions a teacher may want to consider while listening to student discussions might include the following:

- Did I select activities that directly increased student understanding of the unit focus questions?
- Did the design of the performance task allow students full opportunity to demonstrate their learning?
- What improvements should I make the next time I teach this unit or use this type of performance task?

Compiling and Grading the Unit Folder

When the self-reflection process is completed, it is time to build the unit folder. Throughout the unit, students collect their related information and assignments in the appropriate section of their three-ring binders. They assemble these *in sequence* according to the table of contents created for the unit.

They place the papers in a student-made folder with the following grading criteria written on the inside cover: *neat, complete, on time,* and *organized.*

The student earns one point for each of these criteria met. *Complete* and *organized* are determined by the presence and order of papers matched to the table of contents. The final score is then tallied; we equate a score of 4 with an A, a score of 3 with a B, and so on. We follow the same grading procedure as used in grading the actual performance task.

1. Student partners first determine another student's folder grade by simply counting up the points they have given the folder during grading.

2. The folder is returned to the owner for self-assessment and possible appeal.
3. The teacher makes the final grade determination.

Parent Review and Conference

Now the unit folder is ready to be sent home for parent review. The parent is asked to review the folder and comment in writing on the student's performance throughout the unit, paying particular attention to the unit performance task. The folder is then returned to school to be placed in the student's portfolio.

In preparation for parent conferences, students review their self-reflections from unit performance tasks and other portfolio pieces that demonstrate their progress. This prepares them to write a self-evaluation for that grading period that conveys an insightful picture of their current abilities and achievements.

Using their self-evaluation and work from unit folders and portfolios, students—from second grade on—can sit between their parents and teacher and actually direct the conference by showing parents the work they have produced. Students are able to present an accurate picture of their learning to both their parents and their teacher because of their complete involvement in the learning and assessment process.

We have found student involvement in the conference to be tremendously beneficial, increasing the positive interaction between parents, teacher, and students. By being an active part of the communication during the conference, students realize there is no mysterious information being exchanged during the conference between parents and teacher. Students are present to hear and be a part of valuable feedback firsthand.

Reader's Assignment: Complete your own self-reflection about each of the end-of-chapter assignments. What did you discover? What will you do differently next time?

Benefits of the Model

Our approach to the entire instructional process—even after 20 years of experience as classroom teachers—has been revolutionized by this method of assessment. Students who are involved so completely in the assessment process begin demonstrating genuine pride in their work. There is a shift in the overall classroom atmosphere: No longer must the teacher be the primary catalyst for motivating students to do well. Students now become genuinely excited and motivated as a result of their own participation in the decision-making process.

Jane Cimolino, the consummate teacher and mentor mentioned often in this book, served as one of the original team members who developed this assessment process in the year before her retirement. She had thus used this model of assessment only in its beginning stages. Yet in evaluating the model's impact on her own instructional effectiveness, she had this to say: "Isn't it interesting that after 35 years of teaching—and just when I'm ready to retire—I finally got it right?"

Benefits to Students

After continually refining this model, we have noted several benefits to students.

- Expectations are clearly defined and understood by all.
- The grading process is no longer a mystery to students.
- Involving students in setting standards results in their understanding the characteristics of quality work.
- The level of personal responsibility for learning grows.
- The quality of individual and group work increases over time.
- Students have the tools to become successful, and they use them.
- The unit content is constantly reviewed through the peer- and self-assessment process.

Students award high marks for this system of evaluation. Victor, a special-education student who earned many A's during his sixth-grade year, said,

> Rubrics are like sheets that help you decide how much effort you want to put in. If you want to put in a little effort, you get a C. If you want to put in more effort, you get a B. And if you want to put in maximum effort, you get an A.

Jessica, a student identified as gifted, shared this:

> I like rubrics because I know what my goals are. At my old school, my teacher just gave my paper back with a grade, and I didn't know why I got that. It's easier for the class to get better grades because we know the criteria for getting an A, B, or C. I'm kind of afraid that next year in junior high they won't have rubrics and my grades will drop because I won't know what I need to include on my essays and stuff.

Ryan, who hopes to become a geneticist, said,

> Having the class making rubrics is a lot better than the teacher just grading your paper. If you make a mistake on an essay or something, you don't know what is wrong, so you don't know how to correct that the next time you do an essay. But with a rubric that you helped make, you'd know what was wrong with it. Then the next time you could do it right and get a better grade.

Involving students in developing criteria to evaluate their work benefits a much wider spectrum of the school community than merely students themselves. Teachers, parents, and administrators also gain valuable insights with regard to student learning, instructional methods, and curricular emphasis.

Benefits to Teachers

There are many benefits to teachers using a student-centered assessment system.

- Clarifying instructional objectives provides structure for students.
- Focus questions make instructional choices easier.
- Instructional objectives, instructional activities, and the performance task are aligned.
- Student discussions and self-reflections provide the teacher with useful feedback about instruction.
- Increased student engagement increases student motivation and participation.
- Observing students during peer assessment provides valuable insights regarding student learning and group interactions.

Teachers complete an evaluation following their participation in our student-generated rubric workshops. Following is a sample of reactions we have received from teachers.

> Valuable tool for learning because it truly empowers students and clarifies for the teacher as well. I have used these strategies in small doses and definitely have been motivated to keep pursuing them. I'm really excited again! Thank you! —*Assessment Academy workshop participant, Chula Vista, California*

> Appropriate assessment for all grade levels. Even my little ones at grade one have done minirubrics. The nonreaders are paired with a reader to do assessments of writing. The nonwriters will draw and label their reports for assessment. —*first-grade teacher*

> Your workshop was *outstanding*! I am anxious to try student-generated rubrics. We have this huge "state fair" we do (in lieu of the traditional fifth-grade state report). This year we are adding a multimedia component

utilizing the Internet and working in conjunction with the computer-lab teacher. We are going to try this rubric method and hope for the best. This is a powerful assessment tool. *—Kathy Wiebke, fifth-grade teacher, Sonoran Sky School (Paradise Valley, Arizona)*

This was an excellent workshop! I really learned a lot today. Thank you! I want to try using this rubric method with my second/third-grade combination class. I have a much better understanding of using a student-generated rubric in a primary classroom. Thanks again! *—Trish Diaz, teacher participant*

Benefits to Parents

Once parents become familiar with this alternative assessment process, they recognize that it benefits them in many ways.

- They understand the requirements of an assignment and can better assist their child in its completion.
- They know ahead of time how their child's work will be assessed because the class-created rubric is sent home when the performance task is assigned.
- They understand how their child's grade was determined when the graded paper or project is brought home.
- They know what content their child is actually learning.
- They have a more complete picture of their child as a learner.

Here is a sampling of feedback we have received from parents.

Great presentation! As a parent, I want student rubrics in every class in every school. These rubrics will be just as important for parent use. No more helpless feelings when working with our children. I love teaching children personal responsibility for their own learning. They will teach themselves to be successful learners—lifelong. What a buy-in! *—parent invited to staff-development workshop for teachers*

Partner-grading is a great idea! I'm really interested in that. I also liked the emphasis on continual striving for quality. As a parent, this program works well for me, makes a lot of sense, and seems easy to understand. *—parent of student using this model in a classroom*

Benefits to Administrators

We have had many conversations with school, district, county, and state administrators involved in assessment who have attended our presentations. Numerous benefits of this model have been identified by administers.

- Additional assessment information about students beyond standardized test data is provided.
- Communication among teachers regarding priorities of the instructional program is improved.
- Schoolwide standards and grade-level expectations are developed.
- Overall quality of the school's academic performance increases.
- Consistent standards are established schoolwide for instruction and assessment programs.

School administrators recognize that this assessment model has great potential for building a schoolwide assessment program. This is a sampling of the feedback we have received from principals, following our professional development workshops with their staffs.

Teacher's comments were overwhelmingly positive. It was exciting to listen to teachers discussing what they have already implemented. Your presentations were all I expected and more! *—Marilyn Erickson, principal, Haskell Math-Science Technology Magnet School, Los Angeles Unified School District (Granada Hills, California)*

Our school will be undergoing a Program Quality Review this year, so these strategies for assessing and analyzing student work are especially important to us now. All our teachers, including the special-education staff, are finding that this helps them to have a clear understanding of what students really know. *—Rosemary Enzer, principal, Danube Avenue Elementary School, Los Angeles Unified School District (Granada Hills, California)*

Our staff is beginning to use rubrics in the classrooms. They are experiencing true amazement at the results in student work. *—Sandi Carter, principal, Castle Heights School, Los Angeles Unified School District (Los Angeles, California)*

A final word sent to us by another school administrator sums up the educational value of the student-generated rubric model of assessment.

Wow! Absolutely fabulous presentation! You make me miss teaching sixth grade. The opportunities for students to rise to our expectations are what we should always look for in each classroom. Students can be empowered to be responsible for their own learning, heightening motivation and interest, therefore making them lifelong learners. *—Martha Villafranca, principal, Otay Elementary School (Chula Vista, California)*

13 Frequently Asked Questions

We hope you are excited about using this assessment program with your own students in your own classroom. You may, however, have some questions. These are the ones we hear most often in our workshops.

Can kids really learn to become objective assessors of their own work and that of their classmates?

Absolutely. We have found that students can become objective assessors provided they receive sufficient training and modeling. Students are carefully taught to look for specific content and criteria matched to the rubric they've created. This assessment process is objective, and therefore students can use it effectively. The more students work with this model, the more successful they become at grading.

Isn't this process too time-consuming?

At first, it may seem like it. As with learning anything new, it does take more time initially. But once the teacher and students have worked through the process a couple of times, it is much less time-consuming. You'll find that the results gained in terms of student learning, level of participation, and quality of work more than justify the investment of time.

How can I inform parents about this process?

An ideal opportunity to introduce this program to parents is during your back-to-school night presentation at the beginning of the school year. We suggest you use the Summary of the Assessment Process (given in blackline-master form on page 104) in your presentation. If the year has already begun, you might consider holding a special session for parents just to explain this aspect of your instruction and assessment program or send home a letter. We have prepared a sample parent letter summarizing the process (see page 105), which you might want to adapt or distribute to your own parent community. Once you and your students are comfortable using this assessment model, you may want to invite parents in to watch students creating rubrics and assessing their work.

Are students with special needs successful using this model?

This model practically guarantees success for all students if they are willing to take responsibility for their learning. We recognize that students with special needs often require additional assistance to meet assignment expectations. We have found that these students actually do better with this model because both the performance task and the criteria to assess it are very clearly defined. This enables parents, resource teachers, and other instructional-support personnel to better help students succeed. When these students see themselves as able to meet the same expectations as their peers, their own level of confidence and motivation increases.

I have a class of students this year that seems to be more immature and less responsible than classes I've had in prior years. Any suggestions for using this model with them?

The key here is to provide your students with more structured training. You will have to walk them through the process more thoroughly than you would with other classes. Try first applying this model to classroom-behavior standards or following directions. As students make the connection between the rubric and their own performance, you can begin applying the model to academic work. Guide them until they demonstrate the ability to carry out the necessary steps independently. Be patient. You will see the results you want if you persevere.

Do you allow students to redo their unit performance task after the initial assessment?

The answer to this question is a qualified *yes*. We believe primary students should always be allowed to redo their work if they are motivated to do so. Teachers of upper-grade students, however, might consider deciding this on an individual basis rather than making it a class policy. Certain students seem to need that extra step to experience success, especially when they are first introduced to this process; parents are happy that their child is given the opportunity to improve. Keep in mind, however, that the ultimate goal is for students to be able to follow directions and complete the task correctly the first time it's assigned.

How often do you use this type of in-depth assessment? Is this your only method of evaluating student progress?

We use this method of assessment only with major projects or end-of-unit performance tasks. It is important not to *over-rubricize*—a term we coined that means writing rubrics too often. Remember, this is only one part of a balanced assessment program. Other, more traditional assessment measures are necessary to provide you with a complete picture of students' progress and abilities.

Reader's Assignment: Make a list of the questions you have about implementing student-generated rubrics as you work through the process. Brainstorm some answers alone or with another teacher and try them out. You will make this system your own by experimenting and finding what works best for you.

14

A Staff-Development Model

In our workshops with teachers, we are always looking for ways to present this information in a relevant and useful way. We especially want all teachers to see this model as a valuable addition to their own individual instructional programs.

If implementing this program in individual classrooms results in dramatic student progress, imagine what could happen if this model were implemented schoolwide! There would be an ever-increasing benefit to students involved in this type of assessment program throughout their consecutive years of schooling. These students would become more capable of shaping their academic destiny with the tools they have been trained to use.

We believe the critical foundation on which students learn to self-evaluate by comparing their own performance to the directions given for an assignment is laid in the years from kindergarten through second grade. The benefit to primary teachers is that students naturally become responsible for upholding classroom expectations by having many opportunities for self-reflection.

By the time most students reach the second half of third grade, they are ready to transition into simple, objective, peer-assessment activities (for example, checking off items on the rubric to indicate that directions were followed). As fourth graders, these same students are able to further extend their experience with peer assessment by learning how to identify content and quality in their own work and in the work of others.

The groundwork done in kindergarten through fourth grade prepares students for the more sophisticated work of participating in the full peer-assessment process by the time they reach fifth and sixth grades. Students in seventh and eighth grade can generate task-specific rubrics for each individual academic subject area and effectively participate in the peer- and self-assessment process.

Individual School Training Model

Typically, our workshop is an intensive one- or two-day training session in which teachers learn strategies for practical and immediate implementation of the student-generated rubrics assessment model. To illustrate the power of this assessment model, teachers are shown samples of fifth- and sixth-grade students' work in language arts, social studies, science, and math. We also show samples of primary students' work matched to rubrics students created with their teacher. Teachers see how the foundation of the instruction and assessment model is built in the primary grades and forms the basis for further development in the upper grades.

In our all-day workshops, teachers

- identify the focus questions for a unit
- determine a performance task for that unit
- work in teams to design a rubric to assess the performance task
- collaborate and share teacher-generated rubrics with the full group
- discuss applying the model to a unit currently being taught
- practice assessing student work using the task-specific rubric (usually during the second day of a two-day session)

A three-day workshop, which is summarized below, is even more effective when training an individual school staff.

Day One All teachers and the site administrator receive training in the first phase of the assessment process. Here is a summary of what we do during the first day.

1. Present an overview of and rationale for the model.
2. Show the concept applied to the classroom setting with actual focus questions, rubrics, and student work.
3. Ask teachers to practice creating their own language arts and math rubrics in grade-level teams.

4. Suggest teachers self-reflect to determine how they will begin applying the model in their own classroom programs.
5. Give teachers the homework assignment of meeting with their grade-level teams within the next week to accomplish these tasks.
   a. Select a unit—one they are familiar with—that all teachers in a grade level agree to teach.
   b. Write focus questions for that designated unit.
   c. Select a performance task to assess students' understanding of the focus questions.
   d. Write a rubric with your own students to evaluate that task.

Once all grade-level team members accomplish this, they meet as a team to share their rubrics and their experiences writing those rubrics with their students. They then teach the unit and meet with us to receive training in how to grade the performance task.

Day Two All teachers meet with us on the second day of the training to learn how to lead students through the assessment of the completed performance task. Teachers bring student work and the accompanying rubric to this session. Using their own students' papers, they learn how to conduct peer assessment and self-reflection according to our model. Teachers then return to their classrooms to involve students in evaluating the same performance tasks.

When all the tasks have been evaluated by both students and teacher, the teachers again meet with their grade-level teams to discuss their experiences with the assessment process. They prepare a list of several firsthand discoveries or insights gained through this process to share at the third and final day of training.

Day Three This day is split into two parts. In the first half, we ask each grade-level team to informally share with the rest of the staff their unit focus questions, rubrics, samples of completed performance tasks, and list of discoveries they have made. A discussion of important issues that surface from the sharing follows.

The final assignment we give the teachers is to develop a plan to use the model in an ongoing way in their own classroom programs. In this self-reflection activity, we pose questions to the teachers such as

- In which subject area and unit within that area will you next apply this model?
- How will you improve the use of this model with your students?

The key to the successful implementation of this model on a schoolwide basis is the ongoing involvement of all teachers. However, to increase the effectiveness of the training process, each grade-level team selects a team leader who acts as a liaison between the consultants and the grade-level teams.

During the second half of this day, these team leaders and the site administrator meet with us to design a performance-assessment program for the entire school based on an area of targeted academic focus. We then outline the procedures they can follow to implement this program.

A Suggestion for Districtwide Training

To implement this model of assessment districtwide, a core of teachers and administrators well trained in this process would be responsible for the staff training at the individual school sites. Each school would establish a site-assessment team made up of a building administrator and four classroom teachers. These steps would enable an entire school district to use this assessment model.

1. All site-assessment teams meet with consultants for three days of training in which teams receive an overview of the assessment model, write task-specific rubrics, and learn to train students for peer assessment.
2. At the end of the third day of training, site teams are given the assignment to return to their schools and conduct training based on the individual school training model described above.
3. Teams meet again with consultants to share the results of working with their own teachers at school sites. They discuss issues raised during this

first phase of implementation. Consultants guide participants through the development of a districtwide performance-assessment system in the targeted curricular area.

4. Teams return to sites and help their staffs use the model to teach and assess an additional unit of study. This important step allows the site-assessment team trainers another opportunity to further solidify the implementation of this model within their school.
5. The site teams meet one final time with the consultants to devise a districtwide plan for the continued use of the model.

If you are interested in having your staff or district receive training in the use of this model of assessment, you may contact the authors at the following addresses:

Larry Ainsworth
265 Country Haven Road
Encinitas, CA 92024
(760) 944-3563
mrateach@sdcoe.k12.ca.us

Jan Christinson
1769 Avenida Vista Labera
Oceanside, CA 92056
(760) 945-0977
jchristi@sdcoe.k12.ca.us

15 Sample Focus Questions, Performance Tasks, and Rubrics

In this final chapter, provide the reader with one or more rich examples of the alignment of instruction and assessment for each grade level (K–6). The elements of the model for each example contain this set of components:

- Focus questions or assignment directions
- A performance task based on the focus questions
- A student-generated rubric used to evaluate the performance task
- A corresponding sample of student work
- An evaluation

Example 1

Grade Level Kindergarten

Assignment Directions Show you can draw three pictures—one each for the beginning, middle, and end of a story.

Performance Task After listening to *Goldilocks and the Three Bears* read aloud by the teacher, students will draw three pictures, one each for the beginning, middle, and end of the story. They will use three colors in their drawings.

Rubric	
Happy Face	**Straight Face**
• Three pictures show what Goldilocks does at the beginning, middle, and end of the story. • Pictures are in order. • Three colors are used. • You did your best, neatest drawing.	• Something is missing. • Pictures are out of order. • There are only one or two colors. • Work is not neat.

Evaluation This paper earns a happy face because it has three pictures that relate to the story and it uses three colors.

Example 2

Grade Level One

Assignment Directions

1. Show that you can add using a pattern.
2. Show your answer to an adding problem using pictures and words.

Performance Task If one chicken has two legs and one tail, how many tails and legs do three chickens have? Explain (using pictures, words, and numbers) how you got your answer. (Adapted from *Ventura Unified Mathematics Sampler K–12,* sixth printing, by Ventura Unified School District. Reprinted by permission.)

Rubric		
Star	**Happy Face**	**Straight Face**
• Correct answer using pictures, numbers, and words • Written or oral explanation of answer	• A reasonable answer using pictures, numbers, or words • An attempt at a verbal explanation	• Any answer using pictures, numbers, or words

Evaluation This paper earns a star because it is the correct answer. It has pictures, numbers, and words that explain the answer.

Name Barbara M. Grade 1 Date 11/5/96

Teacher Chang School Kelly

Chickens

If one chicken has 2 legs and one tail, how many tails and legs do 3 chickens have? 3+3+3=9

Explain how you got your answer. I counted my fingers

Example 3

Grade Level Two

Assignment Directions Show that you understand how ones, tens, and hundreds work together.

Performance Task Draw a picture to show how ones and tens are regrouped. Then draw a picture to show how tens and hundreds are regrouped.

Rubric		
3	**2**	**1**
• Picture has words, pictures, and numbers. • Reader can understand how ones, tens, and hundreds work together. • Pictures are about the math in the problem.	• Picture has words, pictures, and numbers. • Reader can "kinda" understand how ones, tens, and hundreds work together. • Pictures are about the math in the problem.	• Picture has words, pictures, and numbers. • Reader cannot understand how ones, tens, and hundreds work together. • Pictures are *not* about the math in the problem.

Evaluation This student's work earns a 3. It has words, pictures, and numbers. The reader can understand how ones, tens, and hundreds work together.

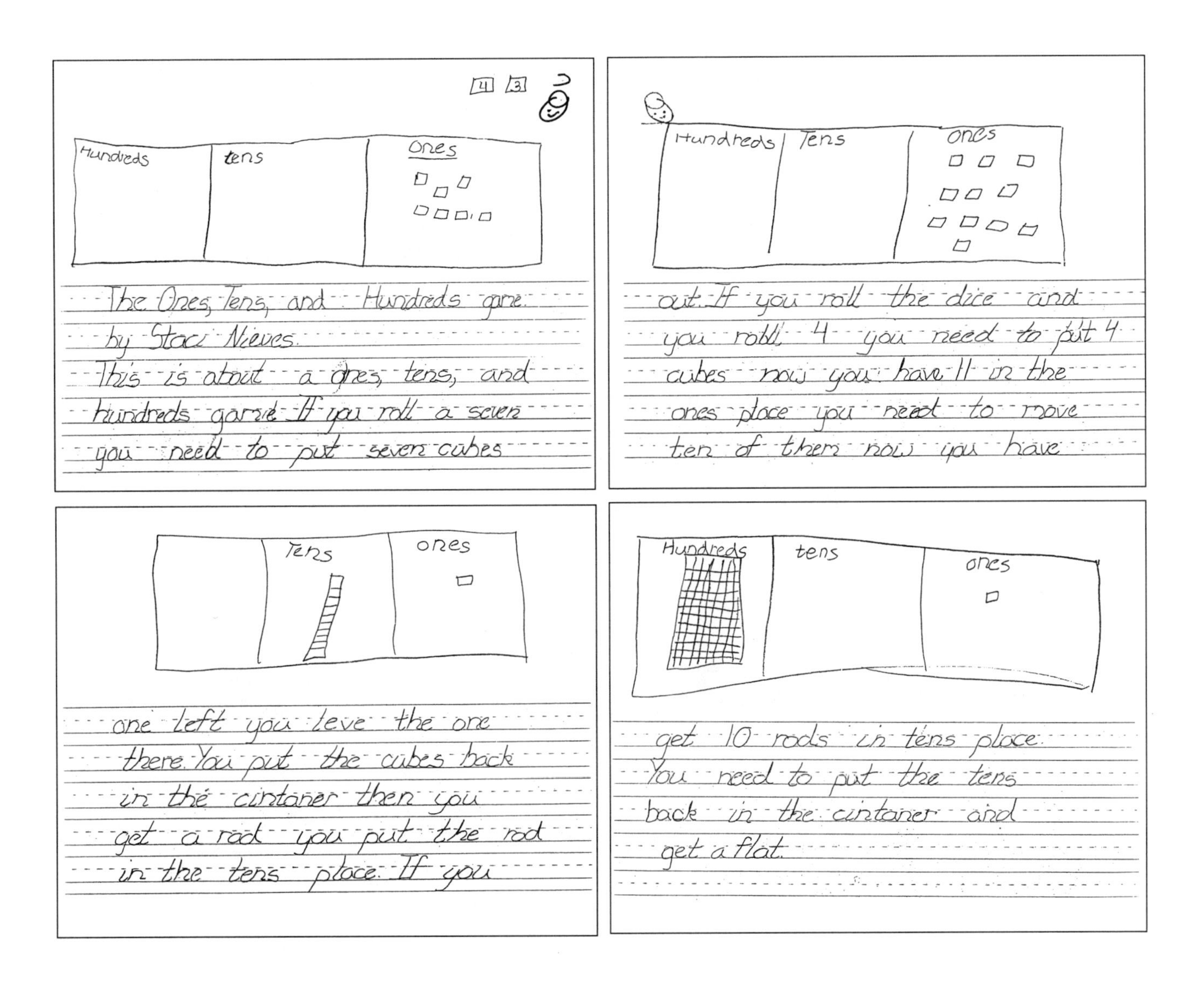
4
3
Hundreds
tens
Ones
The Ones, Tens, and Hundreds game
by Staci Nieves.
This is about a ones, tens, and
hundreds game. If you roll a seven
you need to put seven cubes
Hundreds
Tens
ones
out. If you roll the dice and
you roll 4 you need to put 4
cubes now you have 11 in the
ones place you need to move
ten of them now you have
Tens
ones
one left you leve the one
there. You put the cubes back
in the cintaner then you
get a rod you put the rod
in the tens place. If you
Hundreds
tens
ones
get 10 rods in tens place.
You need to put the tens
back in the cintaner and
get a flat.

Example 4

Grade Level Three

Assignment Directions

1. Show that you can correctly identify the four major regions of California.
2. Show that you can describe the plants, climate, land, and animals of the state region you choose.
3. Use alliteration in the title of the state region.

Performance Task Design a travel brochure to show the different regions of your state (in this example, California). Include a map with a key that correctly identifies all four regions. Include a paragraph description of each of the following: plants, climate, land, and animals.

Rubric

1	2	3
• Title • Student names • Four pictures • At least one sentence included in each description (land, plants, animals, climate) • Map on front	All 1 criteria plus • Four detailed pictures • At least two sentences included in each description • Neatness • Detailed map	All 2 criteria plus • Three or more sentences in each description • Colorful, detailed map • Big, bold title

Evaluation This student brochure received a 3 because it has all the criteria listed on the rubric to earn a 3.

The Mysterious Magical Mountains
winter
summer
KEY
Mountains
Deserts
Valleys
Coasts
Niki M.
Austin M.
Zachary F.
Taylor R.
Climare
Usually in the winter it is cold and wet. They useally get lots of rain. About 20 inches or more fall a year in the mountains. In the summer it is sunny and warm. Also in the summer it is very humid.
LAND
he mountains are topped with snow. The mountains are also at high altitude. The valley is pretty lumpy because of the mountains. The sights are beautiful from the top of mountains. There are also fresh water streams everywhere. You can even hear the streams from far off.
Plants
John Muir said, the Mountains had wild gardens. he wanted to save California's forest. The pine trees get very big and very green. There are scrubs, too.
Animals
There are different kinds of mammals in the mountans. There are: mountans lions, grizzly bears, bats, wolves, rabbits, deer, brown bears and sqarrels. There are fish, in the rivers. The different kinds of birds include: owls, eagles and smaller birds.

Example 5

Grade Level Four

Assignment Directions Show that you can mix and match to find all possible combinations when given a group of items.

Performance Task Sam's Deli has four kinds of bread (rye, wheat, white, and sourdough), three kinds of filling (ham, turkey, and cheese), and two kinds of toppings (mayonnaise and mustard). If each sandwich has only one kind of bread, one filling, and one topping, how many combinations of sandwiches could Sam's Deli make? Show your work and tell why you have all the combinations. (Adapted from *Ventura Unified Mathematics Sampler K–12,* sixth printing, by Ventura Unified School District. Reprinted by permission.)

Rubric		
A	**B**	**C**
• Has correct answer • Shows all possible combinations • Explains why you are sure you have all possible combinations • Uses words, pictures, and numbers	• Has reasonable answer (not exact number of combinations, but close) • Gives incomplete list of combinations (missing up to five) • Has incomplete explanation • Uses words, pictures, and numbers	• Has unreasonable answer (many combinations not found, which lowers final number) • Gives incomplete list of combinations (missing six or more) • Has incomplete explanation (missing words, pictures, or numbers)

Evaluation This student paper is an A paper because it meets all A criteria in the rubric.

1 white ham, mustard
2 white, ham, mayo
3 White, turkey, mustard
4 White, cheese, mustard
5 White, cheese, mayo
6 White, turkey mayo

1 Wheat, ham, mustard
2 Wheat ham mayo
3 Wheat, turkey, mustard
4 Wheat, turkey, mayo
5 Wheat, cheese, mustard
6 Wheat, cheese, mayo

more on back →

Sour dough, ham, mustard 1
Sour dough, ham, mayo 2
Sour dough, turkey, mayo 3
Sour dough, turkey, mustard 4
Sour dough, cheese, mustard 5
Sour dough, cheese, mayo 6

1 rye, ham, mustard
2 rye, ham, mayo
3 rye, turkey, mustard
4 rye, turkey, mayo
5 rye, cheese, mustard
6 rye, cheese, mayo

There were 6 sandwiches for every kind of bread and 6x4=24

6 + 6 → 12
+6 +6 → 12
24

THE END

Example 6

Grade Level Five

Focus Questions

1. How and why did people come to North America?
2. What evidence do we have for our theories?
3. How and where did the land bridge form?

Performance Task Write a three-paragraph essay and draw a map that answers all three focus questions about the land bridge.

Rubric		
A	**B**	**C**
• Complete freehand map • Map labeled correctly • Focus questions answered completely (according to content required)	• One major item incomplete (focus questions or map) • Everything else complete	• Two or more major items incomplete

Evaluation This paper is an A paper because it meets all A criteria in the rubric.

Land Bridge Test

① During the ice age, Indians came to North America from Asia many years ago. They came over on a landbridge known to us as the Bering Strait. Now the Bering Strait is very far under water but then it was a strip of land over the ocean. The Indians came here wile hunting for food and finding a spot to build a new home but didnt realise they were in North America.

② The folowing is a list of evidence for our theories:

- similar languages of Native America
- Same blood type of Native America
- preserved footprint of a cild in mud
- writings on the caves of walls
- cup shape on the back of Native Americans teeth
- spear point in rib of extincted ice age animal

③ The land bridge formed between Northern Siberia and North America. The land bridge was a stripe of land formed by glaciers. During the Ice age the water from the ocean evaporated into clouds. The clowds rained over the mountains and frose into glaciers because it was so cold. During the short summers the snow and ice had no time to melt so eventualy the ocean kept evaporating and freezing that the water level droped 300 ft and uncovered land.

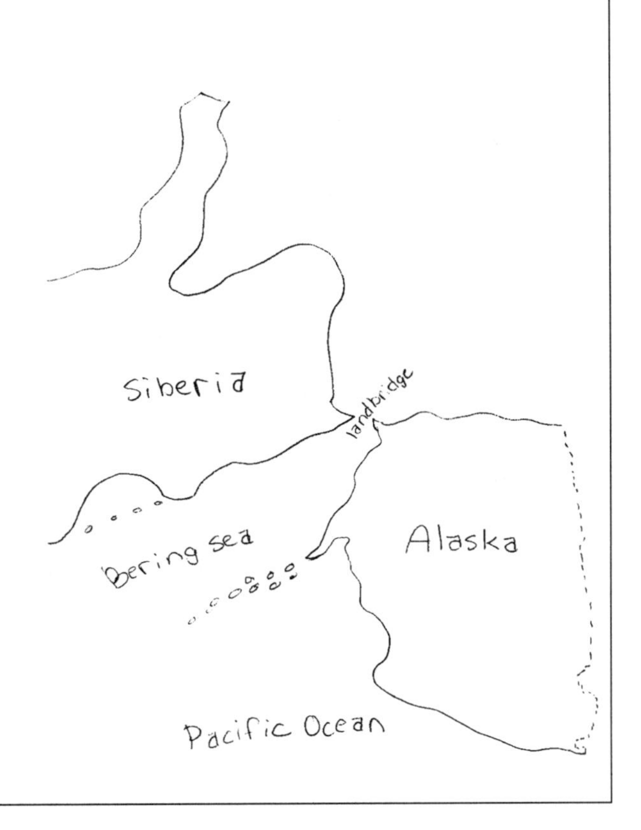

Example 7

Grade Level Five

Assignment Directions

1. Use rates to find a particular term in a series of rates.
2. Use rates to find the best buy.

Performance Task Using the concept of rates, decide which of the following box of raisins would be the best buy. Design a poster to prove your answer.

Rubric			
A	**B**	**C**	**D**
• Has correct answer • Gives clear verification of answer • Is organized like a poster • Is complete and neat	• Has correct answer • Gives clear verification of answer • Could be neater and better organized • Missing minor item	• Has incorrect answer • Gives unclear verification of answer • Is not neat—doesn't look like a poster	• Has incorrect answer • Is incomplete—major items are missing • Didn't follow directions

Evaluation This student poster is an A poster because it meets all the A criteria in the rubric.

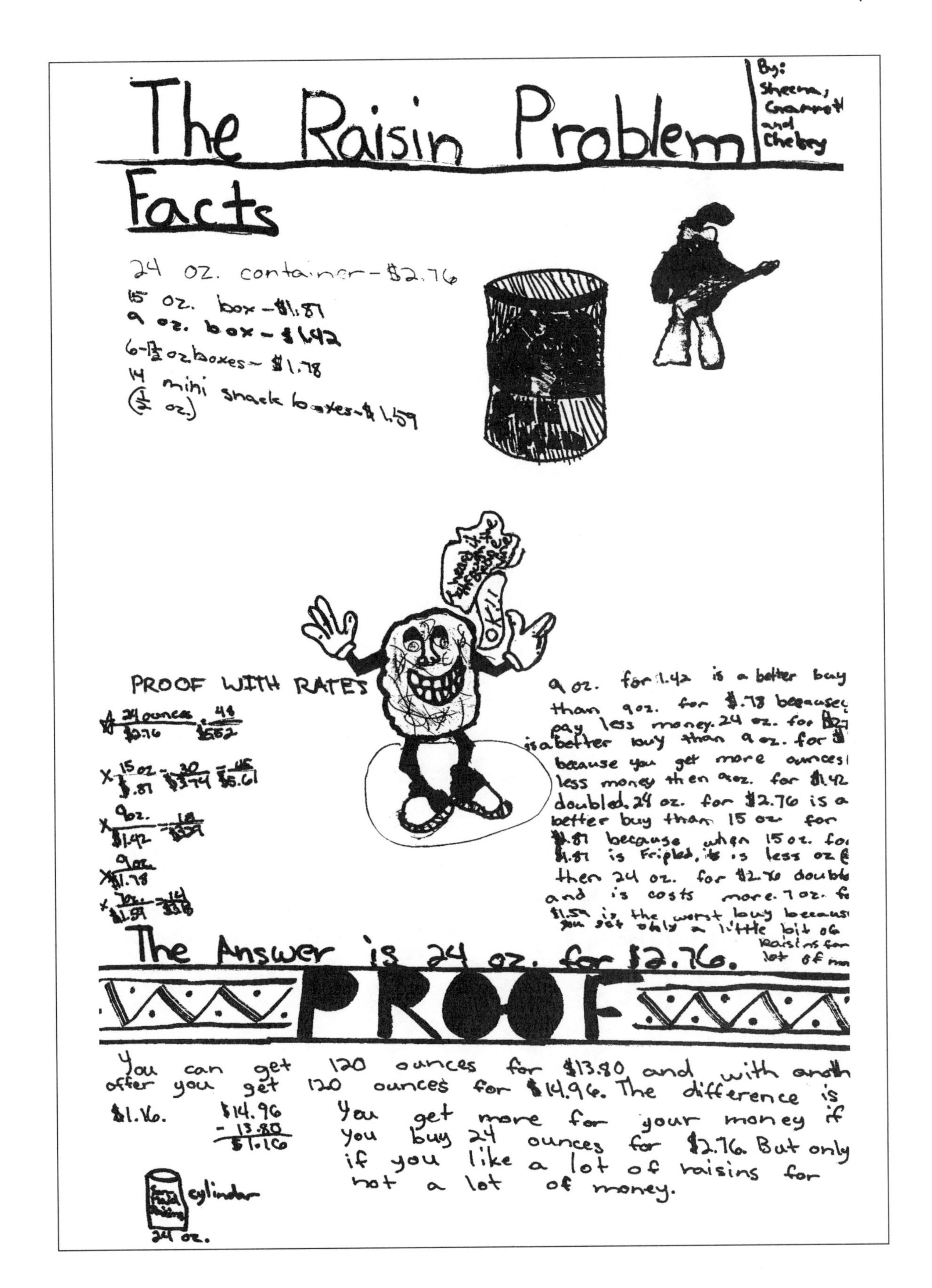

The Raisin Problem
By: Sheena, Garrett and Chelsey
Facts
24 oz. container–$2.76
15 oz. box–$1.87
9 oz. box–$1.42
6-1/2 oz. boxes–$1.78
14 mini snack boxes–$1.59 (1/2 oz.)
OK!!
PROOF WITH RATES
9 oz. for 1.42 is a better buy than 9 oz. for $.78 because you pay less money. 24 oz. for $2.76 is a better buy than 9 oz. for $1.42 because you get more ounces for less money then 9 oz. for $1.42 doubled. 24 oz. for $2.76 is a better buy than 15 oz. for $1.87 because when 15 oz. for $1.87 is tripled, it is less oz than 24 oz. for $2.76 doubled and is costs more. 7 oz. for $1.59 is the worst buy because you get only a little bit of raisins for lot of money
The Answer is 24 oz. for $2.76.
PROOF
You can get 120 ounces for $13.80 and with another offer you get 120 ounces for $14.96. The difference is $1.16.
$14.96
- 13.80
$1.16
You get more for your money if you buy 24 ounces for $2.76. But only if you like a lot of raisins for not a lot of money.
cylinder
24 oz.

Example 8

Grade Level Six

Focus Statements

1. To become familiar with the biography genre of literature
2. To read a biography and write a summary of the person's life
3. To correctly identify the elements of a biographical work
4. To report on the person's life in poetry format

Performance Task Create a 10-line bio-poem on a poster according to the following criteria:

Line 1	Person's name
Line 2	Four traits
Line 3	Related to . . .
Line 4	Who cares deeply about . . .
Line 5	Who feels . . .
Line 6	Who needs . . .
Line 7	Who gives . . .
Line 8	Who fears . . .
Line 9	Who would like to see . . .
Line 10	Resident of . . .

Decorate the border of your poster with symbols or scenes important to the person's life.

Rubric		
C	**B**	**A**
• Name, date, and title of the project author • Bold title and author • All 10 lines of description • A border with a couple of pictures or words • Five to seven spelling and mechanics errors • Neat, readable, bold writing (printed, cursive, or typed)	All C criteria plus • All 10 lines with descriptive writing • Color or detail in border, words, and drawings • Insight into person's life • Three to four spelling and mechanics errors	All B criteria plus • Neat and readable bold writing on the borders (wherever this applies) • All-round detailed description • Colorful and detailed drawings or words • Statement of why person was important or famous • Two or fewer spelling and mechanics errors • Pictures explained with captions (if needed to understand)

Evaluation This bio-poem meets all the A criteria.

Example 9

Grade Level Six

Focus Statements

1. To understand the elements of advertising (appealing to interest of consumer, giving facts needed to make a decision in bold, easy-to-read format)
2. To design and create a poster to advertise a favorite book you have read

Performance Task Design a poster to advertise a book of your choice. Include on the poster the title and author of the book, your name, a summary of the story, your favorite part of the book copied in quotes, a description of the main character(s), and your recommendation. Be creative in your design and arrangement of the required information.

Rubric

C	B	A
• Title, author, your name • A summary of the story • Your favorite part of the book copied in quotes • A recommendation of the book • Description of main character(s) • Labels for each section • 5 to 7 spelling or mechanics errors	All C criteria plus • Short interest grabber (easily seen) to hook the reader • Eye-catching words or pictures • A detailed summary • Detailed pictures of main character(s) • 3 or 4 spelling or mechanics errors	All B criteria plus • Detailed picture of setting • Color on pictures, titles, or labeled sections • 0 to 2 spelling or mechanics errors

Evaluation This work earns an A because all criteria needed for A are there.

Dealing With Dragons
A beautiful princess...
And a charming dragon...
What happens?
Written by,
Patricia C. Wrede
Main Character:
Cimerone...
is the 7th daughter of a royal family. She doesn't care about her proper life until she meets tl dragon Kazul.
Main Character: Kazul...
is a charming dragon who needs a princess just like Cimerone.
Summary:
Cimerone is a princess who decides to runaway because she's fed-up with her royal life. She volunteered to be the dragon Kazul's princess. She finds that being a dragon's princess is much more exciting than it was at home. She finds some wizards snooping around and she knows that they're up to no good but doesn't know what they are up to. After lots of snooping she finds that the wizards are going to cheat to help the dragon Woraug become the King. If Woraug becomes King he will give the wizards the magic crystal ball. What can she do? Will Woraug become the new King?
My Favorite part:
" 'Cimerone!' Alianora hissed, clutching at Cimorene arm, 'There's someone behind that bush!' "
Recommendation:
My Opinion of the book is it gets two thumbs-up! On a scale of one to ten, I give it a twelve. I loved this book!
A book that once you start you can't put it down!...
-Booklist
A good book for anyone looking for adventure...
-New York Times
Keeps the reader hooked...reads like a whirlwind...
-Washington Post
Setting:
Megan Taylor

Example 10

Grade Level Six

Focus Statements

1. Solve word problems correctly in different math strands
2. Communicate an understanding of the process followed to solve a problem
3. Be able to verify the answer through mathematical reasoning

Performance Task Solve the Problem of the Week. Use the Problem of the Week Guide to produce a data sheet and write-up of the problem.

The student work shown is in respose to the Problem of the Week called "The Whimsy Factory." The Whimsy Factory sells widgets. These widgets are placed in 2 sizes of boxes. The smaller box holds exactly 7 widgets, and the larger box holds exactly 13 widgets. An order comes in for 125 widgets. How many boxes of each size are needed to package the order exactly?

Rubric			
A	**B**	**C**	**D**
• Follows the Guide completely. • Data sheet is complete; no further explanation is needed. • Paragraph 1 of the write-up includes all the information given in the problem. • Paragraph 2 includes specific math steps and math vocabulary. • Paragraph 3 includes correct answer and verification.	• Answer is correct. • Follows the Guide. • Data sheet shows how problem is solved, but the solution needs more explanation. • Specific math steps are missing in the write-up. • Verification doesn't prove the answer.	• Answer is incorrect *or* answer is correct, but write-up doesn't show how the problem was solved. • The Guide wasn't followed completely.	• Answer is incorrect. • One or more sections required on the Guide are missing.

Evaluation This student's work shows all A criteria including the correct answer, and it follows the Problem of the Week Guide.

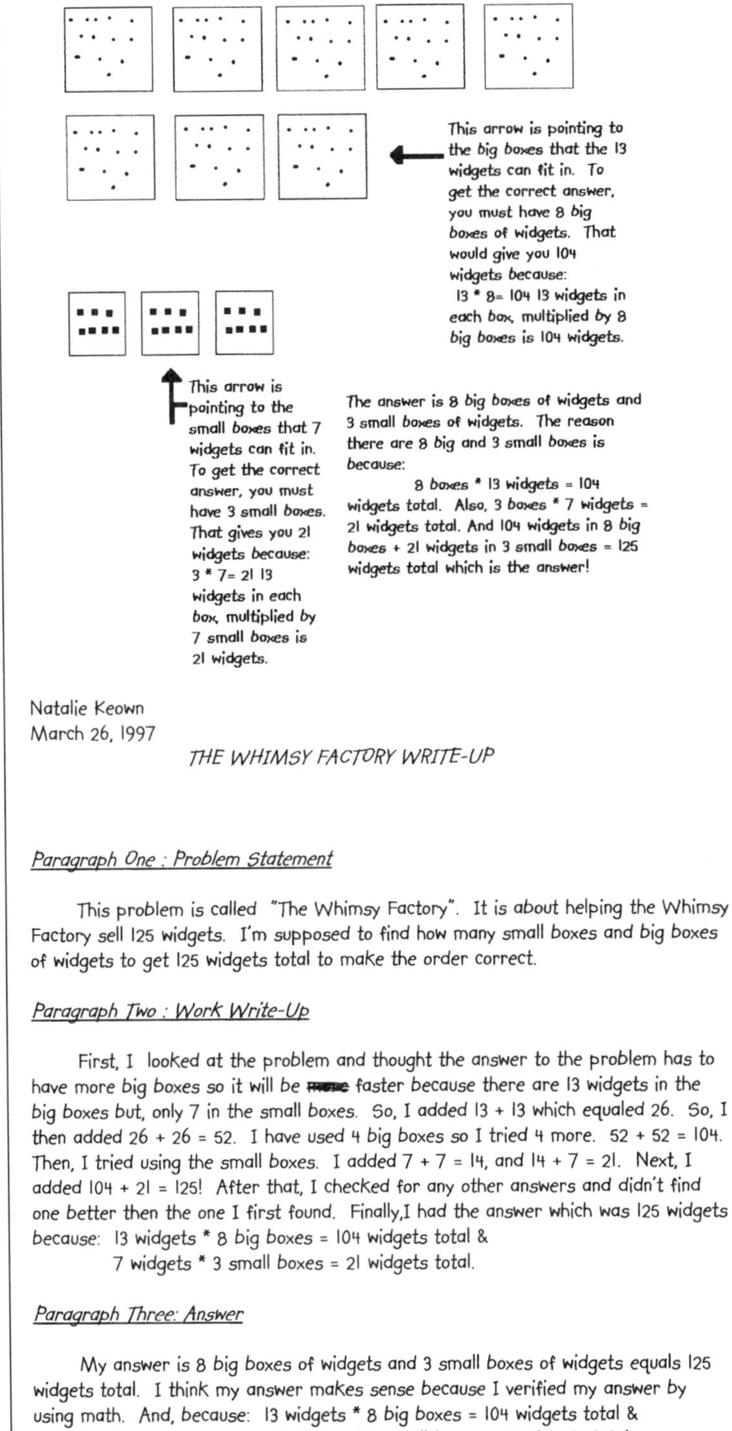

This arrow is pointing to the big boxes that the 13 widgets can fit in. To get the correct answer, you must have 8 big boxes of widgets. That would give you 104 widgets because:
13 * 8= 104 13 widgets in each box, multiplied by 8 big boxes is 104 widgets.

This arrow is pointing to the small boxes that 7 widgets can fit in. To get the correct answer, you must have 3 small boxes. That gives you 21 widgets because:
3 * 7= 21 13 widgets in each box, multiplied by 7 small boxes is 21 widgets.

The answer is 8 big boxes of widgets and 3 small boxes of widgets. The reason there are 8 big and 3 small boxes is because:
8 boxes * 13 widgets = 104 widgets total. Also, 3 boxes * 7 widgets = 21 widgets total. And 104 widgets in 8 big boxes + 21 widgets in 3 small boxes = 125 widgets total which is the answer!

Natalie Keown
March 26, 1997

THE WHIMSY FACTORY WRITE-UP

Paragraph One : Problem Statement

This problem is called "The Whimsy Factory". It is about helping the Whimsy Factory sell 125 widgets. I'm supposed to find how many small boxes and big boxes of widgets to get 125 widgets total to make the order correct.

Paragraph Two : Work Write-Up

First, I looked at the problem and thought the answer to the problem has to have more big boxes so it will be faster because there are 13 widgets in the big boxes but, only 7 in the small boxes. So, I added 13 + 13 which equaled 26. So, I then added 26 + 26 = 52. I have used 4 big boxes so I tried 4 more. 52 + 52 = 104. Then, I tried using the small boxes. I added 7 + 7 = 14, and 14 + 7 = 21. Next, I added 104 + 21 = 125! After that, I checked for any other answers and didn't find one better then the one I first found. Finally,I had the answer which was 125 widgets because: 13 widgets * 8 big boxes = 104 widgets total &
7 widgets * 3 small boxes = 21 widgets total.

Paragraph Three: Answer

My answer is 8 big boxes of widgets and 3 small boxes of widgets equals 125 widgets total. I think my answer makes sense because I verified my answer by using math. And, because: 13 widgets * 8 big boxes = 104 widgets total &
7 widgets * 3 small boxes = 21 widgets total.

Blackline Masters

Summary of the Assessment Process

Teachers write focus questions.

Teachers choose a performance task aligned with the focus questions.

Teachers design unit activities to match the focus questions and performance task.

Teachers inform students of the focus questions and performance task.

Teachers build a rubric with students and send a copy home to parents.

Teachers teach the unit.

Students complete the performance task.

Students peer assess and self-assess the performance-task projects.

Teachers review students' work and determine the final grades.

Students engage in self-reflection.

Work is sent home for parent comments.

Parent Letter

Dear Parents,

I am writing to tell you about a grading system that your child will participate in this year. The goal of this system is to take the mystery out of the grading process and increase student responsibility for learning. To accomplish this, students help determine how grades are defined and then take part in grading projects. Because students are involved, they understand the grades they receive.

Whenever I begin a new unit of study or a major project, I share with students the three or four major ideas I want them to learn from the unit. Next, I tell students about the end-of-unit project, which will give them the opportunity to show what they have learned. To determine how the projects will be graded, students and I work together to create a *rubric*—a specific set of descriptions for each letter grade that tells what must be included to receive that grade. This rubric guides students as they work on their projects.

When the projects are done, students use the rubric to evaluate their own work and the work of their peers. I review the student grades and make the final grade determination. Then students reflect on their progress during the course of the unit and share their unit folders with you.

I have found that this assessment program gives students several valuable benefits. When students help decide the standards of work quality, they learn what quality work looks like. And when students clearly understand what the expectations are, their level of personal responsibility for learning increases. Finally, since the unit content is continually reviewed throughout the grading process, students retain more. I hope you will see evidence of these benefits, too.

Before a project is due, your child will share with you the rubric to tell you how a unit project will be evaluated. This will help you monitor and support your child during the completion of the project. Your child will also show you the final project and the evaluation, including a self-evaluation.

I welcome your questions and comments. Please do not hesitate to contact me for further information.

Sincerely,

Name ______________________________ **Date** ____________

Self-Reflection Form

1. How well did you learn the information necessary to answer the focus questions for this unit? Explain.

2. Discuss how you did on the performance task for this unit. What are you pleased with? What could you have done better?

3. What is your specific plan for improvement? What will you do differently next time?

Rubric and Grading Form

Grade Point	Grading Criteria

Peer graders ______________________ and ______________________

Grade _______ Justification ______________________________________

____

____

Self-grade _______ Justification ______________________________________

____

____

Teacher's grade _______ Comments ______________________________________

____

____

Problem of the Week Guide

Follow these directions exactly to create a data sheet.

1. Write your student number, your name, and the date at the top of a piece of paper. Write the title of the Problem of the Week with the words *Data Sheet.*
2. Show all the work you did to solve the problem using words, pictures, and numbers.
3. Write a concluding sentence at the end of your data sheet that clearly states the answer to the problem.

On a separate page, record your write-up.

1. Write your student number, your name, and the date at the top of this piece of paper. Write the title of the Problem of the Week with the words *Write-Up.*
2. Copy the paragraph titles shown below, and use the sentence starters provided to complete your write-up. Everything you write must refer to the math content, the procedures you followed, and the strategies you used to solve the problem. You can print, type, or use cursive writing. Write in paragraph form.

Paragraph One: Problem Statement	Paragraph Two: Work Write-Up	Paragraph Three: Answer
This problem is about . . . I am supposed to find . . .	Explain step-by-step and in detail everything you did to complete your data sheet and arrive at your answer. Think of it as a recipe for someone to follow or directions to your house. You may include strategies you used that didn't work. First I . . . Then I . . . Next I . . . After that I . . . Finally I . . .	Verify, or prove, your answer by referring to the math you did. Don't write that you checked it on the calculator, you did it twice, or a friend told you. My answer is . . . I think my answer makes sense because . . .

Problem of the Week Rubric

A	B	C	D
• Follows the Problem of the Week Guide completely. • Data sheet is complete; no further explanation is needed. • Paragraph 1 of the write-up includes all the information given in the problem. • Paragraph 2 includes specific math steps and math vocabulary. • Paragraph 3 includes correct answer and verification.	• Answer is correct. • Follows the Problem of the Week Guide. • Data sheet shows how problem is solved, but the solution needs more explanation. • Specific math steps are missing in the write-up. • Verification doesn't prove the answer.	• Answer is incorrect *or* answer is correct, but write-up doesn't show how the problem was solved. • Problem of the Week Guide wasn't followed completely.	• Answer is incorrect. • One or more sections required on Problem of the Week Guide are missing.